Selecting and Implementing Energy Trading, Transaction, and Risk Management Software

A Primer

Catalog-in-Publication Data

Patrick E. Reames and Dr. G. M. Vasey
Selecting and Implementing Energy Trading, Transaction, and Risk
Management Software – A Primer
ISBN 1-4196-8829-4

Design by Inreason Media
www.inreason.com

Printed in the United States of America

First Edition 2008

Selecting and Implementing Energy Trading, Transaction, and Risk Management Software

A Primer

Authored & Edited by

Patrick E. Reames

Vice President, Trading and Risk Management

UtiliPoint International, Inc.

&

Dr. G.M. Vasey, Ph.D.

General Manager, UtiliPoint Europe

UtiliPoint International, Inc.

Table of Contents

Dedication

To all our friends and associates in the energy industry.

and

To Julie and Allison – *P. R.*

FOREWORD

Jon T. Brock

President & COO, UtiliPoint International, Inc.

I am pleased to present the second UtiliPoint 'Expert' Series book on selecting and implementing energy trading, transaction and risk management software. The first book in the series, focusing on ETRM software products, has proven to be tremendously popular and this new follow-up, providing an in-depth look at the activities that are most critical for any company acquiring ETRM products, is a valuable addition for anyone involved in the energy trading and risk management space.

UtiliPoint bases much of what it does as an analyst and consulting firm on both its proprietary research and the expertise of its staff. This book benefits from both. First, over the past 4-5 years, UtiliPoint, under the direction of Dr. Vasey and Mr. Reames, has undertaken some 15 proprietary research studies in the area of ETRM software including market sizing, trends and benchmarks, integration and implementation. The benefits of performing proprietary research are that end users, suppliers and selectors of ETRM software gain knowledge about how their peer group has undertaken and approached various tasks including what types of experiences they have had with their software. While UtiliPoint publishes many of its findings in the accompanying reports, the analysts involved in the projects actually learn much more about the industries use of ETRM software than can be written in a report. This data, benchmarking and current knowledge of trends and issues is what

3

sets UtiliPoint apart from our competition and allows us to provide our clients with informed quantitative and qualitative insights.

The second component is the use of experienced analysts and staff. As Mr. Reames and Dr. Vasey write about ETRM software, selection and implementation, they do so as not as observers, but as accomplished experts in their own right. Mr. Reames has overseen more than one hundred ETRM implementations in his previous roles as both executive and delivery expert at ETRM software vendors and has developed methodologies and approaches to implementation for those vendors. Dr. Vasey has also worked in senior roles for ETRM software vendors, has overseen ETRM implementation projects, developed methodologies and approaches and ran large project teams.

It is this combination of genuine expertise from practical everyday application and UtiliPoint's array of proprietary research data and analysis, notwithstanding their performing the role of analysts day in, day out, that shines through in the pages of this book. These experts bring not only experience and knowledge of the space, but do it fully informed by utilizing research and data gathered in their analyst activities.

In addition to our own internal expertise, we have leveraged that of our sponsors, Deloitte and Touche LLP, Sapient, and The Structure Group. These are companies that are involved in the "heavy lifting" of ETRM every day at client sites around the globe. Their contributions to this book provide you a wealth of true "thought leadership" in energy trading and risk management. We are truly grateful for their contributions and their support in making this book a reality.

We believe the result is that this book truly is one of an UtiliPoint 'Expert' series and we trust that you will find it of value in your endeavors with ETRM software.

Jon T. Brock

President & COO
UtiliPoint International, Inc.

4

SECTION 1

OVERVIEW OF ETRM

CHAPTER 1

WHAT IS ENERGY TRADING, TRANSACTION AND RISK MANAGEMENT SOFTWARE?

Dr. Gary M. Vasey,

UtiliPoint International, Inc.

Energy trading, transaction and risk management (ETRM) software is that category of software applications, architectures and tools that support the business processes associated with trading energy and related commodities. In the broadest sense, energy trading means both the buying and selling of energy commodities such as crude oil, coal, natural gas, electric power, emissions and refined products, the management of the movement and delivery of the energy commodities, and associated risk management activities. ETRM software therefore comprises a broad set of functions that can vary considerably depending on what commodities are traded, what assets are employed in the business, where those assets are located, and what the company's business strategy and associated business processes are.

Usually, and in the broadest sense, ETRM solutions are fully integrated suites of software that help manage the front-, middle- and back-office aspects for an energy trading entity. Although such definitions and organizational structures differ quite widely across the industry, the front-office is usually concerned with deal capture and position management, the middle-office with managing and reporting various risk exposures as a result of trading activities and the back-office with settlements and accounting functions. Additionally, there will usually be at least one scheduling or logistics management component to ETRM solutions that allow the energy company to plan, track, manage and account for quantities of energy that have to be physically moved from its source to some point of usage.

Over the last 2-3 years, UtiliPoint analysis of ETRM solutions has suggested that there are also significant new areas of functionality required by asset-heavy users of ETRM systems such as power generators. These involve various market analysis and forecasting activities including load forecasting and price forecasting in particular regional commodity markets and asset optimization modeling. The requirement is to optimize the use of the assets employed by the business against usage and outage trends in regional markets helping to determine the most profitable way in which to manage those assets given market needs. There is also a real-time trading component to these requirements since adjustments need to be made in real-time through the day as market dynamics change. Another area of functionality required in this industry segment is in market communication; particularly in regional power markets where bidding, dispatch, scheduling, ISO communication, settlements and reconciliations are needed. Figure 2.1 is a simplified comparison of "traditional" ETRM with our view of the emerging need for an Asset-ETRM solution.

Today, many of the larger software vendors in the ETRM space offer comprehensive suites of solutions while other software vendors specialize in market communication, load forecasting and other asset-oriented requirements.

Table2.1 - Requirement summary for ETRM users

Up to the Trade	Moving and Accounting for the Commodity
<ul><li>Deal Capture</li><li>Position Keeping</li><li>Trader Analytics</li><li>Market Data/Analysis</li><li>Risk Analytics</li><li>Risk Reporting</li><li>Counterparty Credit</li><li>Trade Settlement and Invoicing</li><li>Data Mining</li><li>Trading and Risk Controls</li></ul>	<ul><li>Pre-Scheduling/Scheduling/Logistics</li><li>Physical Settlement & Invoicing</li><li>Volume Management</li><li>Reporting</li><li>Market Communication</li><li>Noms/Confirmations</li><li>Asset Management</li><li>Dispatch</li><li>Asset Optimization</li><li>User Decision Support for Optimal Operations</li></ul>
"Speculators"	"Asset Heavy Users"

Although ETRM software functional coverage can be difficult to define, another way to look at it is to consider the types of company that need to utilize ETRM software as follows:

- Hedge Funds trading energy commodities;
- Investment banks trading commodities;
- Energy merchants trading commodities;
- Multinational oil companies trading commodities;
- Producers selling their production;
- Utilities (Investor-owned, Municipal utilities and cooperatives) buying fuel for power generation and for the sale of wholesale gas or electric power;

- Local Distribution Companies buying wholesale energy to sell to retail markets;
- Large commercial and industrial end users of energy;
- Petrochemical and refining companies that procure feedstock in wholesale markets.

Given the list of different segments of the energy industry that might require ETRM software, it can be readily understood that the required functionality of such systems can be very extensive and complex.

Another way to think about ETRM software is to consider the management of two primary functions across these entities. First is the business of managing the assets employed in the business (whether those assets are generation facilities, produced quantities of oil, gas or electric power), and secondly the merchant function that is involved in the buying and selling of commodities and managing associated risks. ETRM software is used to manage the merchant function and but increasingly it has to be integrated with and/or include asset management functions.

It is very difficult to define the entire functional coverage of an ETRM system simply as a result of the different variations in requirements at the detailed level. However, on a broad level, the software will comprise most of the following applications or functions;

Front-Office Applications

Electronic Trading

The resurgence in electronic trading has benefited those that survived including Intercontinental exchange (ICE). However, electronic trading is utilized by a variety of industry players that conduct trades and those trades need to be captured in the ETRM system so as to insure that it is the primary system for position keeping and risk management.

Deal Capture

The deal capture application area supports the traders and/or administrators capture of deals into the system for further processing. Generally, deal capture is the start of the transaction flow through to invoicing but it usually requires other set up data to function correctly such as contract and counterparty data. Deal capture requires a high level of ease of use to allow traders and administrators to enter deals rapidly. Many vendors have therefore developed "deal blotter" screens in addition to long-form deal capture screens. The deal blotter screen looks and behaves like a spreadsheet and is a familiar work environment for traders. Additionally, it may often be configurable allowing a specific trader to 'default' many of the data items on the screen for more rapid data capture.

Deal capture systems need to be able to capture any number of transactions - both physical and financial. It is this that adds to the complexity of deal capture systems since each deal type requires any number of additional and unique attributes to be also entered. One issue that may arise with the deal capture function is in capturing physical and financial deals in different systems. Financial deals may sometimes be captured in a risk system while the physical deals are captured in the transaction management systems. This results in a need to link corresponding deals and can lead to integration and position keeping problems.

As the industry has evolved, the deal capture business function has become more standardized, with better definition of the instruments and deal types used across the industry. In turn, this has allowed vendors and solution providers to develop better solutions to support traders. Nonetheless, deal capture can be a complex piece of functionality especially if it is combined with trader tools for what-if analysis and if it is required to provide instantaneous valuation and risk measures such as Value at Risk and Mark to Market valuation.

Despite the increased standardization in this business function, since it is often provided as a module in a broader-based solution, it is rarely deployed stand-alone. In almost all cases, the deal capture module is bundled with other functionality to provide transaction processing through pre-scheduling and often to invoice.

There are many ways in which deals get done today including over the telephone, through an exchange, using Interactive Messaging and email. All of these different media have to be captured in the ETRM's deal capture area.

Real-time Trade Capture

For any power company with generation, real-time trading also has to be performed and those deals captured in the system. Real-time trading is conducted to maintain balance as generation operations progress and as real-time needs arise on the grid and it is a separate function from the actual wholesale trading operations that deal with time periods beyond the day of operations. Real-time trading is therefore more typically a requirement for utilities and generators than merchants and often managed by the regulated arm of the company.

Trader Analytics

Analytic tools to support traders in their activities have become common additions to many ETRM systems in recent years. These tools can include price calculators (option prices, etc.) as well as "what-if" tools allowing traders to analyze the impact of a trade against a portfolio. One evolution that has taken place in the analytics area is one from models developed primarily for financial markets to more energy-specific models that take account of the specific behavior of the underlying commodity.

Position Keeping

Position keeping is the function that essentially tracks trades and their offsetting physical and financial positions and has long been an area of short coming in many trading/marketing departments and systems. Despite the fact that most third-party packages provide some position keeping functionality, many trading floors still rely on manually update whiteboards and spreadsheets to keep overall position. The issue is partly about the diversity of systems used by marketers/traders and the lack of a coherent integration framework that can bring all the required data together and present it in a usable form and, partly related to business process shortcomings – particularly where deals are entered after the fact. Position is required in multiple formats. For example, overall portfolio position, position at various points on the grid as well as physical and financial position. It is this level of complexity that has kept position keeping a largely manual activity in many marketing/trading shops.

Scheduling Applications

Pre-Scheduling and Scheduling

Scheduling involves organizing planning and tracking the movement of physical energy commodities via some transport mechanism and for that reason scheduling systems have different functionality depending upon the commodity to be scheduled and the geographic location in which the movement will take place. Scheduling or pre-scheduling is another function that can be extremely complex and that many vendor-provided solutions still fail to address completely. In North America, gas scheduling comprises pathing, nominating, and confirming gas volumes through various pipelines whereas electric power scheduling involves pathing power through various grids and communicating back and forth with the regional power markets. Scheduling for other commodities such as crude oil and coal may involve utilizing barges, trains, trucks or vessels and the tracking of those shipments from one place to another.

Scheduling is a function that both plans the movement of the commodity but also tracks and accounts for that movement. So for example, a company may plan to move a volume of natural gas along a pipeline but it needs to have the legal right to do so and then communicate back and forth with the pipeline on issues such as the actual volumes delivered and shipped, the transportation costs and any losses in volume that take place on the pipeline and so on. It is a very complex function and different solutions are required for each commodity and geography.

eTagging & ISO/RTO Interfacing

These functions are important in scheduling electric power in North America and as the interfacing and e-tagging requirements are largely regional (by ISO or RTO) in nature, this business function has not and might never truly standardize in North America. It therefore provides a niche opportunity for specialist solution providers. The function involves communicating to the regional power market operator using

13

its standards for data interchange as well as reconciling and settling on the actual quantities that moved.

Middle-Office Applications

Risk Management

Risk management systems in the energy industry became essential tools after wholesale power markets opened up. The instantaneous nature of power, its lack of storage capabilities, and price volatility drove the adoption of risk management across the industry. The risk system generally captures financial trades directly and then provides various exposure reports for both financial and physical trades/portfolios.

Many risk systems provide a variety of tools to value trades, books, and portfolios including Value at Risk and Earnings at Risk. The diversity of instruments/trades that need to be represented in risk systems may include weather, interest rates, and foreign exchange transactions as well as energy commodity related instruments. Risk system vendors are now adding methods and reports to address aspects of the physical side of the business such as volumetric and deliverability risk. Earnings at Risk and similar tools are an example of the shift that has taken place in this area. Earnings at Risk possibly provides a better assessment of how earnings would be impacted by certain events or price movements as opposed to making the assumption that positions can be unwound. For marketers with generation, for example, power is actually taken to delivery and therefore the position cannot be "unwound" in the same way that a financial position might be. This volumetric risk aspect to today's power marketers' business differs considerably to the market risks faced by asset-light merchants.

Another facet of the changing risk management world is the mark-to-market valuation versus accrual accounting often used by utilities. While mark-to-market valuation is a common and accepted method, the difficulty is in understanding how a mark-to-market profit actually gets booked on an accrual basis. Often, traders and marketers have been rewarded based on mark-to-market position as opposed to actual accrued profits. In the past, price manipulation resulted in inflated mark-to-market valuations that after settlement weren't reflected in the company's books, causing apparent profits to "evaporate." As a result, more emphasis is now placed on independent price data but this is difficult in more opaque Over the Counter (OTC) transactions.

Credit Management

Credit management and credit risk management has become an area of concern for all energy companies after the collapse of the merchants and the counterparty credit issues that followed. The credit management function requires access to contract data as well as external credit agency and other credit data. The credit function usually establishes credit profiles for counterparties, monitors credit limits against counterparties as well as manages collateral requirements. It has rapidly become something of a specialized function that has growing importance and is now served by specific credit management application providers.

Additionally, many of the existing ETRM platform vendors also provide some credit management functionality. In this instance, the functionality is usually limited to monitoring trade exposure to counterparties although some systems do go further. Very few traditional trading and transaction management systems however also manage the collateral side of credit management.

With the ongoing emphasis on credit and collateral management as a component of good corporate governance and risk management, this is an area that may see a continued emergence of specialist vendors and a requirement to integrate with existing trading and transaction management systems.

For marketers with both wholesale and retail operations, credit management is a much more complex proposition. If utilizing an ETRM system's credit functionality, this is generally built to provide credit management for wholesale trading activities only lacking the ability and scalability to manage counterparty credit exposure for thousands of retail counterparties. Generally, the solution is to aggregate like contracts into groups and then load those into the credit management module and this again requires external spreadsheets or customized solutions be built.

Additionally, there are developing a number of risk measures such as Credit Value at Risk (CVaR). While some systems ostensibly offer the ability to calculate and report on CVaR, the devil is in the details of the methodology and the ability to enter and store credit data at the appropriate level.

Back-Office Applications

Contract Management

Contract Management data is a key component for trading, credit management and scheduling activities and it is generally provided as a part of an ETRM system. Generally, these systems maintain the key contract data that provides for counterparty credit limit monitoring, transmission terms and trading limits, and so on.

Settlement & Invoicing

While settlement and invoicing are often grouped together, they are two different and important functions. While both functions are often provided by ETRM software packages, many companies actually utilize solutions other than their primary ETRM system to perform these functions. Again, while invoicing is a function provided by many of the primary trading and transaction management systems, but many companies also utilize a different system to produce invoices.

Hedge Accounting

Hedge Accounting has become a mandatory function since the inception of FAS 133 and its equivalent accounting standards. As with credit management, a host of niche solutions has been developed specifically to help perform hedge accounting. At the same time, many traditional vendors have added some degree of hedge accounting functionality to their systems, too.

Other ETRM Functions

Depending upon the type of company utilizing and ETRM system a number of other functions may be required including gas storage, inventory management, generation dispatch, load forecasting, market simulation, stress testing, gas measurement, and more. Additionally, all

ETRM solutions will require some administrative functions including security of access, audit trailing, workflow, interfaces to external price feeds and other external data sources and, document management.

Part of the complexity of ETRM software is that there is no real standard for what comprises an ETRM system. However, as regulations and recommendations are made by various organizations and governing bodies, more standardized approaches are emerging in areas such as risk management, deal capture, and the back office. Still, as the ETRM software class serves such a broad set of essentially niche markets from hedge funds to regional utilities, what actually constitutes an ETRM solution is very variable. It is this that allows so many vendors and products to coexist in the industry since many products are targeted at niche vertical markets or at specific functions within the context of ETRM.

Some ETRM software solutions have gone further in terms of back office functionality too and offer general ledger, accounts payable and accounts receivable functions. However, many energy companies utilize their existing accounting packages to perform much of this functionality requiring an interface between the ETRM system and the accounting system.

The energy industry is actually a very heterogeneous market for ETRM software with horizontal and vertical niches that, on the surface at least, appear to share similar requirements. While many "outsiders" see a large and attractive homogeneous market for ETRM software with good revenue and profit potential, the truth is that there are a plethora of energy company business models and each model has its own detailed version of the same set of requirements. Indeed, at a certain level of detail, all energy companies involved in buying and selling energy commodities have common business functions yet, as you drill down, there are significant and fundamental differences in those requirements. The idea that there are standard functionality requirements is simply a mirage created by a fundamental lack of understanding of the energy business at a detailed level.

Requirements Dictated By Assets and Location

The nature of each energy company's physical assets and the geographic location of those assets actually dictate the majority of the software requirements at the detailed level. The need to record and report on data and transactions is inevitably governed by the regulatory regimes under which the company operates its assets and by the type of assets employed in the business. For example, an electric generator with predominately hydro generation facilities will have different requirements from the company that has predominantly coal-fired facilities. Generators in different geographic regions will have different reporting requirements. During the energy trading bubble, the fundamental importance of assets was overlooked and the recent return to asset-centric trading has increased the importance of asset-related software requirements.

Summary

It is difficult to define ETRM software precisely. At its core, ETRM software comprises deal capture, position keeping, risk management, settlement and invoicing along with some scheduling modules organized such that data is entered only once and flows through the system from the front office to the back office. In reality, each company using an ETRM solution has its own particular requirements and each vertical market niche from production to Local distribution requires some variation in functionality and some extensions to functionality. Indeed, it is this variability in requirements that adds to the overall complexity of implementing ETRM software.

CHAPTER 2

THE ETRM SOFTWARE LANDSCAPE

By Dr. Gary M. Vasey,

UtiliPoint International, Inc.

&

Mr. Patrick Reames,

UtiliPoint International, Inc.

The ETRM software space has evolved rapidly in step with the industry and its requirements since FERC Order 636 effectively created the category just 15 or so years ago. ETRM software vendors and products alike have arrived and then disappeared again in response to the volatility of the energy trading industry and this is discussed in detail from a historical perspective and using UtiliPoint's 'dislocation model' in our book *'Trends in Energy Trading, transaction and Risk*

Management Software – a Primer' (BookSurge Publishing, 2006). But since that book was written, many more changes have taken place in the space.

The market for ETRM software has rebounded significantly since the merchant collapse and it is now a vibrant and dynamic industry. New entrants from the financial sector including hedge funds, proprietary traders and investment banks, as well as de-regulation in Europe, has fostered explosive growth in energy and other commodities trading. The maturing of electronic marketplaces such as ICE and NYMEX has in effect also reduced many of the barriers to entry for those wishing to trade commodities and the expansion of the number and type of instruments to trade has fueled this growth. Another aspect of the growth in ETRM software markets has also been simply that requirements have changed and, particularly in North America, the need to replace older solutions has also grown.

With respect to this latter point, UtiliPoint has established both market maturity and replacement rates in the North American and European ETRM software markets. In North America, studies (UtiliPoint International, Inc., 2006) support the fact that the last 2-3 years has seen increased procurement activity with 26% of study respondents stating that they had last purchased a system in 2004/5. However, there were a number of older systems still installed among the respondents including systems which were originally procured in the 1996-1997 timeframe. About 30% of the respondents in the study said they had plans to procure a new ETRM system in the near future and an equal amount did not know. 30% is high and suggests that ETRM software demand will remain high for at least the next two years; barring any unforeseen industry issues. Additionally, those with plans to procure new software were either replacing homegrown solutions or buying a package for the first time (virgin market) or, were about to replace an older solution (replacement market). What's interesting about this data is that it is the first to indicate that the replacement market in North America is bigger than the virgin market. Previously, the virgin market component for new purchases was much larger than the replacement market. However, the business drivers for replacing older legacy systems are now more considerable than in the past including Sarbanes-Oxley, corporate governance and a host of other issues.

By contrast and for comparison in Europe (UtiliPoint International, Inc., 2007) the market has a 40% virgin component (i.e. those not using vendor-provided software) which reflects some degree of immaturity as compared to North America however, it is the asset-light segment of the industry that drives this immaturity where more than 50% of all companies surveyed do not use vendor-provided solutions. In other words, the asset-light side of the industry is more virgin than replacement whereas the asset-heavy side is more replacement than virgin. The results also support the fact that the last 2-3 years has seen increased procurement activity with 42% of European respondents stating that they had last purchased a system since 2004. Even home grown solutions are still being deployed and this procurement activity seems set to continue with 23% of respondents planning to procure new ETRM software in the next 12-months according to the survey. In fact, the number may be higher because a further 28% said that they "did not know" if their companies had plans to procure new software. So ETRM software markets are booming on both sides of the Atlantic and this increase in sales activity has not been lost on those observing the market.

M&A Activities

M&A activity has also boomed and seems set to continue. For example, OpenLink acquired IRM AG, SunGard Energy Solutions acquired Energy Softworx and both Global Energy and New Energy Associates were acquired by Ventyx. Additionally, Triple Point Technology acquired India based developer CoralGrid Software, Ltd. Recent acquisitions in the ETRM space clearly indicate that many solution providers are moving to broaden their presence outside of the "traditional" ETRM model, seeking to service an ever increasing portion of the energy value chain. While the market for wholesale energy trading and risk management systems remains strong, areas adjacent to this market are showing similar strength and have drawn the attention and dollars of the ETRM vendors.

Competition among the leading vendors, particularly in the "asset light" market (deals involving hedge funds, banks, and brokers) has been fierce. As that segment of the industry and the software products servicing it mature, it is becoming increasingly difficult for solutions providers to differentiate themselves from their competition for these primarily financial players. Sales in this segment are becoming more about the vendors' reputations and less about the products functionality. However, for prospects holding significant assets, such as generators, utilities, and oil and gas producers, logistical and physical risk management challenges offer solutions vendors an opportunity to sell a combination of creative products focused on solving these unique and complex problems.

SunGard Energy's acquisition of Energy Softworx enabled the company to broaden their market reach without having to expend significant resources on product reconciliation. Energy Softworx has achieved success by focusing on unique logistical problems and in the process has become the market leader in the servicing of fuel management needs for power generators. Their FuelWorx product, with additional modules covering fuels budgeting, rail management, and gas fuel supplies, is a targeted solution that provides deep functionality in areas that are underserved by "typical" ETRM solutions. With this acquisition and the transition of the ACES power scheduling and deals management system onto the Entegrate platform, SunGard is now able to offer a broader asset oriented solution to merchant generators and utilities.

In January of 2007, Open Link Financial announced they had acquired IRM, a European based provider of asset management, forecasting, optimization and planning solutions for utilities, generators, and oil and gas producers. While primarily serving the European markets, OLF has indicated that they are bringing the IRM solutions to the North American market and are focused on growing their presence in the asset heavy space. Their asset centric strategy is further evidenced by their recent announcements of the release of a new oil and gas producer services module and *cMotion*, a logistics and scheduling solution for virtually any commodity.

Solarc, a company that has seen significant success in the natural gas liquids, petroleum, and industrial fuels markets with their RightAngle product, announced that they picked up Trinity Apex, a provider of physical gas management solutions. Trinity Apex's Ties II product provides significant gas producer, transportation, and storage functionality, giving Solarc a wider footprint in the physical natural gas markets.

The acquisition of Global Energy Decisions and New Energy Associates by Ventyx (created by the merger of Indus International and MDCI Mobile Data Solutions) now positions Ventyx to cover the majority of the power utilities value chain from generation to retail billing and customer care.

Triple Point's acquisition of CoralGrid gives the company new capabilities in the precious metals markets and opens up additional opportunity to sell Triple Points other solutions to CoralGrid's primarily financial and banking clients.

Moving Toward Energy ERP

ETRM vendors are taking a more holistic view of the energy markets—not only acquiring products covering adjacent functionality, but also creating new ones, such as OLF's producer module. Certainly, ETRM will continue to be a lucrative market for these vendors, but areas such as asset management, forecasting, and planning and control are commanding more attention and becoming components of more comprehensive energy solutions.

Customers Impacts

For systems providers, the advantages of serving the wider energy markets are clear: increased market opportunities and the ability to grow through acquisition without creating product conflict. For the customers of these systems, significant advantages also exist. Integration of the multitude of applications necessary to run an asset heavy business has always been problematic and expensive. Purchasing these systems from a single source helps to shift that burden from the customer to the vendor. Additionally, upgrading components of a single sourced solution should be less burdensome as the newly released products will be compliant with the vendors overall technology and integration framework.

However, downsides also exist. There can be significant risk associated with a single vendor supplying and supporting a majority of systems that businesses rely upon. In selecting a solution covering multiple operational areas, buyers need to be doubly certain that their chosen vendor is stable and has the financial wherewithal to weather potential market downturns. Additionally, the odds are that no single vendor will provide the best "fit" for every need of a complex asset oriented enterprise, leading to some level of compromise in order to get the best overall solution.

Integration Strategies

It is also apparent that vendors are moving towards more emphasis on architecture and integration. The beauty of an increasing focus on architecture and integration is that it starts to make a best of breed selection approach increasingly attractive for users. If the key vendor truly provides an architecture that is configured to ease of integration then that allows the user to deploy point solutions to solve functional issues in areas peripheral to traditional ETRM but it also affords the larger vendors a sense of which point solutions are most successful for partnering more closely with or indeed, acquiring.

Allegro Development was, in our opinion, the first to deploy an architecture that afforded ease of connectivity. Its .Net Service Oriented Architecture is partly responsible for Allegro's ability to win deals over the last two to three years as users recognized that the architecture provided an advantage to them. However, other vendors are at various stages in deploying their solutions on new architectures that carry the same benefits including Triple Point, SolArc, SunGard Energy Solutions, OLF, Navita, and others. It is this fact that will continue to, in part drive M&A activity in the space.

Increasing Vendor Dominance

What is also apparent from the aforementioned UtiliPoint studies is that a small number of vendors and products are becoming more dominant in the space. The top five vendors; OpenLink, SunGard, Allegro, Triple

Point and Solarc are gaining market share faster than in the past by virtue of their broad-based ETRM software platform based on more open technologies and architectures. Notwithstanding this fact, the ETRM landscape remains diverse with around 70 solution providers and while UtiliPoint expects that number to decline, there is every reason to believe that the ETRM marketplace will continue to be characterized by many vendors and products. Why is this?

Despite the fact that there are a number of more dominant players emerging, energy markets are still regional and they are still highly complex. Each type of buyer is also seeking something a bit different in terms of requirements (e.g. a producer requires different functionality to a hedge fund and so on). It is this diversity of requirements – particularly on the physical side of the business where the commodity has to be moved and managed in regional markets – that means there will always be room for regional or market-niche specialists.

UtiliPoint's approach to reviewing the ETRM market is based on market segment, commodity and market tier. This view takes account of some of the complexity inherent in the market and allows us more precision in classifying where the various solutions and vendors fit. While it is true to say that vendor's such as OpenLink, SunGard, Allegro, Triple Point and Solarc are leaders in the space generally, other vendors enjoy dominance in other tiers and market niches such as SunGard Kiodex in hedge funds, TradeCapture in liquids and refined products, Navita and VIZ in certain European markets, The Structure Group in North American market communication, OATI in North American power markets and, so on. There are also niche providers of functionality such as credit risk management such as ROME, niche providers of scheduling software for regional markets and, various providers such as FEA and Lacima of risk management tools.

The fact is that these markets are very complex and regional. This means that there will always be best in class vendors and products serving those markets and in a world increasingly based on more open architectures, a best-in-class approach built around a major vendor's product suite is an increasingly viable and attractive option for buyers. However, this trend also makes it easier for the dominant and cash rich vendors to identify good acquisitions. The ETRM software market will continue to see M&A activity as a result.

European Vendors and New Entrants

There are also a number of European based ETRM software vendors, whose current focus is primarily in Europe, who may become targets for acquisition in the future or may broaden their geographic footprint including Navita, VIZ Risk Management, and others. There have also been some new entrants such as Abacus Solutions with its Saturn product that squarely targets the asset-heavy side of the industry.

Summary

ETRM software markets are maturing. That increasing maturity is evident both in the design and architecture of the vendor's software, the increasing emergence of a handful of more dominant vendors and broader-based solutions and, the nature of the marketplace which is increasingly more replacement that virgin. The increasing maturity of the software market mirrors in fact the increasing maturity of the energy commodity trading industry.

For the buyer, this is good news since it means that there are more viable alternatives in the ETRM software space to chose from that are making it somewhat easier to install a comprehensive suite of solutions that actually have the possibility to talk with one another. In Europe, the landscape is actually richer than in North America, in many respects due to an expanded vendor list that incorporates European vendors. Any one of the products mentioned above can provide users with a good 70+ percent solution to requirements at this stage in their development. The bigger issue for buyers may now not be finding a software solution that can meet the majority of his or her functional requirements but actually getting that product(s) implemented properly!

SECTION 2

SELECTING A NEW ETRM SYSTEM

CHAPTER 3

BEST OF BREED OR SOLE SOURCED?

Dr. Gary M. Vasey,

UtiliPoint International, Inc.

Research by UtiliPoint International has consistently shown that many ETRM solutions in use today actually utilize multiple applications that are integrated or interfaced in one form or another. On average, our research has shown that the total number of applications in use is between 3 and 5 depending on the type of company and number of commodities traded. Of course, the reason for this is the sheer complexity of the requirement, the relative historical immaturity of commercial solutions and the often rapidly changing nature of the business.

Unfortunately for buyers and users of TRM software, at least in the past, no single provider has realistically been able to provide the entire 'soup to nuts' solution – at least not to the level of functionality actually required by the user. Today, that vision is getting somewhat closer to reality. Nonetheless, this issue often leaves companies confronted with a real dilemma when seeking a solution for their energy trading, transaction and risk management business. Whether their total requirement can be met using the software from a single provider or whether to try to architect a solution comprised of different modules and applications from a variety of suppliers. Of course, a custom or partly custom solution might also be considered.

When looking at the vendor landscape it is apparent that there are some vendors that, often using an architecture approach, are seeking to provide, if not a soup-to-nuts solution, then at least a platform that can form the core component of any deployed ETRM solution. There are also many vendors that, seeing the complexity and local nature of some industry issues, seek to focus on delivering a best-in-class piece of functionality that solves just a portion of the overall problem. Over time, it may be that the 'best-in-class' approach vendors are swallowed via acquisition by the platform/architecture vendors but for now both types of vendor exist side-by-side. However, there has been a significant move forward over the last 24-36 months in terms of the architectures used by many major vendors which has made it a little easier to opt for using a primary solution supplemented by some best-in-class applications.

Architectures

Five or six-years ago almost all vendor solutions were essentially client/server-based and somewhat monolithic. This meant that functional gaps in a particular vendors' solution needed to be filled with custom code, spreadsheets or another application – often from another vendor. The issue for the user was then how to interface the different components of the solution. This issue was magnified multiple times by the pace at which vendors released upgrades to their software resulting in a situation where the interfaces were perpetually being upgraded to deal with changes in the interfaced applications - both a costly and time consuming nightmare. However, the issues related to this situation do not end with just the maintenance of interfaces. One of the largest and most significant issues facing IT is data management. Maintaining accurate and timely data is a key activity that can reflect on the business in numerous ways from inaccurate financial reporting through to inaccurate billing and collection delays. Part of the issue is simply volume of data but an additional concern is data ownership. Much company electronic data is generated in individual business functions and stored in application-specific databases while masses of paper data may be filed across the company's departments. Not only is access to accurate data a key concern but reconciling the different versions of data across functions can prove to be both tedious and time-consuming.

In this regard, determining data ownership and "system of record" for data is key along with adherence to internal data management standards. Good data management not only improves the ability to extract timely value for the business to support decision making activities but it also assists in corporate governance efforts. Further, data management is an essential activity in supporting an energy company's brand through accurate and timely interaction with the outside world including customers, business partners and stakeholders.

The migration of IT architectures from the client/server model of the 90s to an n-tier, Web services and object-oriented world both helps and hinders the data management issue. By delivering increased and improved integration capabilities, these architectures are bringing the possibility of improved data management closer to reality. Conversely, the migration to these architectures can be a major undertaking and dependent upon the application vendors own migration plans. Additionally, these architectures provide for improved business processes via embedded workflow and collaboration.

Just how large a problem this is for the industry is aptly demonstrated trough UtiliPoint research. Data from a 2005 study of natural gas marketers and producers in North America[1] shows that only half of

---

[1] Evaluation and Benchmarking of Natural Gas Software Application Usage in North American Energy Companies, UtiliPoint Report, 2005

the solutions in use were vendor-provided (Figure 1) and that most used multiple solutions to manage their business (Figure 2). The same and similar studies by UtiliPoint found that less than half of all ETRM users surveyed had anything other than manual interfaces between these systems.

Figure 1: Origin of ETRM software used by North american producers and marketers of Natural Gas

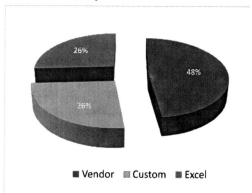

Figure 2: Number of different applications used to manage natural gas trading, transaction and risk management activities by North American producers and marketers of natural gas.

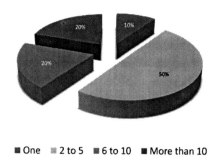

Many of the ETRM vendors have now migrated their application architectures from client/server to n-tier. Although the chosen architectures differ in detail from vendor to vendor, the impact is the same as the new architectures are allowing vendors to deliver solutions that are more flexible, configurable and scalable while also providing significantly improved connectivity via web services for example. These new architectures are having a broad impact on the industry.

The benefits for the end user and the developer of these relatively newly available architectures are substantial but perhaps, most importantly, they provide the built-in connectivity that allows the integration and interfacing issues to be potentially solved. In effect, the new architectures being deployed by the ETRM vendors provide many of the following benefits;

- Provide connectivity that allows integration with enterprise applications, external data feeds and applications and, provides the basis for constructing a true best in class suite of fully integrated ETRM applications;
- Enhances scalability of the ETRM software through the easy addition of additional processing power;
- Provides the basis for the addition of workflow and business process management tools, audit and document management capabilities;
- Allows for enhanced reporting functionality via the addition of a reporting application or using the vendors own reporting capabilities. Some of the vendors are now offering drill-down reporting complete with graphing and mapping features;
- Provides the vendor the opportunity to build in more configurability allowing the package to be customized for each users particular environment and culture thereby enhancing implementation success rates and allowing the vendor to pursue a traditional software vendor business model more easily;
- Enhances the vendor's ability to keep up with industry change by allowing them to break the application up into smaller modules of more discrete functionality;
- Enhances the support and maintainability of the ETRM application.

There are many additional benefits of these architectures including the ability to build data marts and data warehouses from which to perform more analysis.

The implications of the new architectures now deployed by many of the major ETRM vendors is that these applications can be used to provide the core solution while potentially bringing in other vendor's best-in-class applications or developing custom solutions for specific purposes that can be integrated much more seamlessly using the core applications architecture. In reality of course, it's not quite that simple but it's a big step forward from the previous situation.

As some vendors have migrated their current applications to these new architectures and platforms, they have been able to serve their users with more flexible, usable and customizable but supported third-party software. The lack of integration and the risks inherent with that lack of integration seen among marketers and utilities today can potentially be resolved.

Pros and Cons

In order to try to shed some light on this issue, let's initially look at the pros and cons of the different approaches. There is in fact a constant tension between a solution from a single vendor that solves all business problems and provides a consolidated view to the corporation, and the alternative "best of breed" approach that stitches together solutions from different vendors. Both solutions have their merits and downfalls.

The Single Supplier Solution

The single supplier solution attempts to avoid the pitfalls of attempting to integrate multiple point solutions by providing a single solution to all the major categories of applications in one ETRM software offering. This is nice in theory however the requirements of different energy companies are extremely complex and can be quite different in detail. Internally developed projects often tend to end up pursuing this approach too.

Today, many of the larger vendors utilize an underlying architecture that provides connectivity and a host of other benefits and then build point solutions on top of that architecture. The end result is in reality a suite of applications developed on a common architecture stack that work seamlessly together or can be deployed individually.

The Pros of such an approach include:

- Integration, workflow and business process are all fully handled inside the single-sourced solution;
- Only points of integration needing to be considered are those with external systems (external to the ETRM software) and the single solution most likely provides some sort of connectivity via its architecture;
- Everything in the solution is provided by the same vendor and included under the same license and support agreements reducing the administrative burden;
- Testing of new versions of the solution ought to be easier and less costly;
- Training of users is less expensive since the single system utilizes a consistent user interface across the entire application.

The Con's of a single solution include:

- Some functionality might be less than adequate since the application, while broad, might not be very deep in all areas of functionality. In other words, it isn't necessarily best of breed;
- Reliant upon a single vendor to maintain and support the solution;
- In effect created a standard that will require to be invested in over a long time frame;
- Functional gaps might exist now or into the future – how will these be filled?

Best of Breed Solutions

Best of breed solutions are, on the face of it, a great option for all involved. Customers get the benefit of niche products that directly solve their problems, and vendors don't have to support the expense of a massive code base associated with the complete solution. However there are problems with the best of breed approach too. Namely, the customer now has several silos of information that must be massaged and reconciled continually to get any semblance of a smooth business process, and all results must be continually reconciled in order to check that results are accurate. To make matters worse the IT integration expenses tend to be horrendous with popular rules of thumb putting this at 45 percent of an IT budget. For vendors, the situation can be very difficult because they don't have a solution that solves enough of the customer's problems, and so they either get left out of customer selection processes and / or get continually pushed toward creating a complete solution.

The Pro's of a best-of-breed approach include:

- Users have access to the best functionality across the entire ETRM software suite – it is a better fit to requirements;
- Not reliant on a single vendor for product strategy – however, product strategy is now an internal issue;
- Applications are more easily replaced with other best-of-breed applications as requirements evolve.

The Con's of this approach include:

- Necessary to deal with multiple vendors at all times on licenses and support;
- Responsibility for overall product architecture and evolution is internal;
- Requires some sort of architecture strategy or interfacing strategy that can be time consuming and expensive;
- Makes it more difficult to manage product upgrades from each vendor;
- Training users is more difficult potentially since different areas of the system work differently and have different user interfaces and set up.

In reality of course, most companies are forced to adopt something of a middle ground whereby they utilize a single vendor for the majority of the ETRM functionality supplemented by best-in-class applications for specialized activities such as regional market scheduling, market interfaces, asset optimization and so forth. Today, as vendors have adopted an architectural approach to building and deploying their software with built in connectivity, some of the issues of adopting this approach have lessened – but not gone away altogether.

Larger energy companies often utilize the services of a major Systems Integration (SI) firm to help them build a solution. The SI firm essentially takes much of the work of making the solution actually work into their own hands and in the process charges a fee to do so. The usual approach is to utilize one of the major ETRM software platforms as the core solution and supplement it with other vendor-provided or custom solutions on an as needed basis.

Any one of the top 5-7 vendors can today provide a fairly broad-based and comprehensive solution based on a reasonably open architecture. These solutions can meet 80% of business requirements – it is the other 20% that are the issue. These problem areas are most usually local requirements for dealing with particular markets (e bid to bill, scheduling and forecasting/pricing) or related to certain proprietary approaches in risk management or trade management. Additionally, it is a truism to say that the problem of finding a comprehensive single sourced application is larger for energy companies with a large physical aspect to their business and less problematic for more financial energy players.

Summary

The question posed by this chapter cannot be easily answered. Today, many of the more prominent ETRM software vendors have now migrated their applications to architectures that make integration easier but no single vendor has the entire solution for every requirement in the market. While many business practices in trading, risk management and the back office can and have been somewhat standardized the regional and often asset intensive nature of energy trading means that many requirements are also localized or specialized. To some extent, this means that using several different ETRM solutions is almost unavoidable.

For that reason, most companies procuring ETRM solutions may well need to supplement a single sourced solution with a number of other vendor-provided or custom applications. The good news is that by virtue of utilizing newer architectures the integration problem has become just a little easier.

CHAPTER 4

THE RFI/RFP PROCESS

Dr. Gary M. Vasey,

UtiliPoint International, Inc.

When seeking to select new software, most companies will use a Request for Proposal (RFP), Request for Information (RFI), or both. Both documents can be considered to be essential project documents and they should always be carefully and diligently crafted whether they are developed from scratch or are based on a template. Generally, the process begins with the RFI, although sometimes, this step is omitted, especially if the selecting company believes that it has a good basic knowledge of the potential suppliers and solutions in the market.

How Buyers find Vendors

UtiliPoint research has shown that buyers use a variety of means to obtain information on prospective solutions and vendors. Primary sources are the internet and internal colleagues but other sources include software directories, third-parties, tradeshows and external contacts. Perhaps the most interesting finding in the research is the contrast between North American and European software buyers. North Americans will place more emphasis on internal contacts, the internet and software directories whereas European buyers are more likely to obtain information from third-party experts and the internet.

Figure 4.1: Where North American buyers Obtain Vendor Information

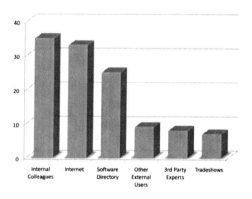

Figure 4.2: Where European buyers Obtain Vendor Information

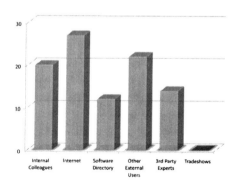

Despite the fact that there are multiple sources to obtain information on vendors and products, to select a product, companies most usually use an RFP driven process. If their knowledge regarding the vendor landscape is pretty thin or out of date they might also do a preliminary RFI.

The Request for Information

The RFI document is generally used at an earlier stage in the selection process to be able to obtain information on companies who can potentially be considered as solution providers or even as system integrators or consultants. Its objective is to simply provide sufficient information on potential suppliers to allow a shortlist to be constructed for the RFP and as a result, it usually seeks a broader and shallower array of information regarding the potential suppliers. An RFI implies no commitment need be made to any responding party, it simply requests information you need to evaluate whether you *might* want to work with a particular company, or *might* want to do a particular project.

In preparing an RFI, the writers should consider both the types of information that they require and how that information will be utilized in making decisions. In the first instance, the RFI will seek at a minimum;

- Basic information regarding the potential supplier including the company's history, general products and services, size in terms of its staff and client base, and how the company is structured;

- Information on the company's financial situation;

- More detailed information on the products and services likely to be proposed as a solution;

- More detailed information on points of contact going forward.

Of course, you can request whatever information you deem appropriate but in general the idea is simply to obtain some basic data with a quick turnaround time for the response. Before preparing the RFI you must ask yourself what you need to know in order to build a short-list of

41

qualified vendors and how you will judge the answers when you receive them. Provide a timescale and desired format for responses too.

Furthermore, the RFI should provide some information regarding the buying entity and its business and requirements at a high level to allow the vendor to make a decision as to whether in fact it should respond at all. A vendor who does not respond or declines to respond is actually saving the prospective buyer time and money by eliminating themselves.

Evaluating the RFI's can be done in a number of ways ranging from purely qualitative through to a quantitative scoring technique. In reality, you may also need to organize additional briefing sessions for the prospective vendors so that they can make queries and it might be invaluable to arrange to meet the vendor's representatives to gain a feel for the professionalism and abilities of the responding vendors. At the end of the day, the idea is, as stated above, to simply come up with a list of vendors that it is felt can meet your requirements (not just functional requirements but also requirements in terms of size, culture, fit and so on).

The Request for Proposal

The RFP will take considerable time and diligence to prepare correctly and the project to build the RFP, issue it and evaluate responses should always be professionally managed by an experienced resource. In most instances the RFP responses can also include vendor demonstrations and quite a good deal of contact with the vendor to allow for questions back and forth for that reason a point of contact should be established.

An RFP implies the probability of a commitment being made to one or more responders. It will include the conditions of your acceptance, the return response format (so all replies are easy to review), confidentiality issues, evaluation criteria, etc. An RFP response should be incorporated into the final contract you sign, as the more specific you make your RFP, the less you will have to negotiate later. It is a good idea to hold a vendor conference shortly after issuing an RFP, so that all responding parties have the same information and get the same clarifications.

Building the RFP/RFI is a critical activity in the selection process requiring significant time and effort. Consideration should be given to a number of requirements in drawing up the RFP including:

- The actual detailed functional requirements for each business process or set of business processes under consideration. Additionally, it pays to understand whether the functionality is essential or simply nice to have. In building the requirements, consideration should also be given to possible future requirements through an understanding of overall business strategy, plans and goals. For example, an electric utility may be seeking a system to manage its power transactions. All current generation may be coal-fired but if its plans include the possibility of building or procuring gas-fired generation in the future as a strategy, what impact might that have on requirements? Having to add natural gas functionality later to support fuel purchasing and management could be a significant expense. Equally, which markets is the company operating in and is that likely to change in the future? If so, does this impact the requirements in terms of a system's ability to interface with other market structures?

- System features and general business requirements ought to be considered including those requirements dictated by Sarbanes-Oxley and FAS 133, for example. Features such as adequate security, audit trails, workflow and document management may also be required;

- IT infrastructure preferences need to be considered to ensure that the software can be cost-effectively supported internally and this category may include whether there is a preference for a traditional license or an application hosting model. It most certainly includes determining the need for integration with other existing systems;

- The vendor's track record, installed base size, culture and overall capabilities to keep the product current, should be taken into consideration when determining vendor preference;

- The vendor should be asked to describe how the proposed solution will be developed, implemented and supported and if it will partner with other companies to provide the solution;

- The vendor should be asked to provide a resourced project plan for the implementation;

- Full and complete quotes should also be provided for all aspects of the project including license fees, support & maintenance, consulting and so on.

Finally, do be realistic about what you actually need in terms of a system and its capabilities by separating the "essential" requirements from the "nice to haves." Over-engineering the requirements will only increase costs and timescales and add to project risk.

In many instances, the requirements can be presented as a list with room for the vendors responses and in all instances, you should be clear about how the vendor's response should be presented. Failure on the part of the vendor to carry out instructions in an RFP can be a useful scoring mechanism when judging responses.

As you prepare the RFP, you should consider how it will be evaluated and scored. This will help frame and organize the questions. You should also consider how much vendor contact you desire and whether to ask for demonstrations during the RFP process or after it with a small number of qualified vendors prior to making a final decision. The scoring and evaluation process will almost certainly require a number of project staff commitments with each bringing a set of expertise to the table.

The vendor's response to an RFP, much like the content of their marketing material, cannot necessarily be accepted at face value. It is not that the vendor intends to mislead simply that they will put their best face forward. Often the vendor's RFP response will contain template components that may be old or make statements that perhaps were once correct but are now not so. The obligation of the project team is to scrutinize the RFP and to test claims and terminology as best they can. An obvious behavioral issue here on the part of the project team is the natural human willingness to accept statements at face value and to look for the answers that were both expected and desired. Caution is required as well as attention to detail to ensure that this natural and normal bias is balanced with the due rigor that needs to be attached to a decision of this importance.

Working with Third-Parties and Template Documents

In many instances a third-party consulting firm is called in to either assist or conduct the selection process. If a third-party is used to help build the RFP/RFI, ensure that it is actually building *your* requirement set and not just tailoring a standard "cookie cutter" template. Template RFP documents have increasingly become a factor in ETRM software selection projects. Standard templates may be a useful starting point but, in this industry, there is no such thing as a standard set of requirements and using a "cookie cutter" approach will only result in extra work and cost along the way and in some cases, failure. While outsourcing the process can be valuable, in the end you cannot outsource the decision!

Two dangers to watch out for in using template RFP documents are as follows;

- Nothing is removed from the template RFP but additional requirements are added leading to an over engineered solution, increased project costs, complexities and timescales. The template RFP requirements should be scrutinized and edited to suit your needs and anything that is really not required should be removed or a least designated a 'nice to have' and not essential.

- The template RFP is based upon the template providers past experiences in software selection and it will certainly reflect that. It should be scrutinized for 'bias' by the user and rigorously amended as necessary since the template RFP and requirements might in reality 'predict' a solution and that solution may be the wrong one.

45

Vendor Software Demonstration

By all means have the vendor demonstrate their proposed solution. Use the demonstration to validate functionality and capabilities as well as to understand how well the software supports the current or planned business processes. The vendor will naturally desire to present the best picture that they can to the selection team and so it is quite safe to conclude that the demonstration represents a better than normal usage situation.

If the vendor arrives unprepared, unrehearsed and the fails to give a convincing demonstration, it should be expected that things may only get worse from there and the vendor should probably be discounted. The vendor's motivation is to prepare, prepare and plan their demonstration to the point that it goes smoothly and shows both them and their software to the best possible degree. Again, it is only human to assume that the demonstration experience will be repeated in real world use. This may well not be the case!

Reference Checking

Of all the methods to find out about your pending partner, this is by far the best. However, it is simply stunning how many companies selecting software never ask for references or, if they do, fail to check them. Remember, the vendor must be expected to provide only their best reference sites and so you should not be surprised to receive favorable responses. Of course, if the references are checked and unfavorable, then this could be a major red flag.

Checking references should not stop there. It is very easy to find out where else a particular vendor is installed. Simply check old press announcements, talk to colleagues and ask the vendor. It is imperative that other sites are checked too! A poor implementation or two is not necessarily indicative of the vendors' suitability but certainly provides a perspective of likely risks and vendor shortcomings to be expected.

Dealing with Bias

One thing that is certain to occur on a selection project is meeting bias. Bias should be anticipated and prepared for and, as much as is possible, decision criteria should be selected that remove bias by being quantitative in nature. Bias can occur as a result of the following types of scenarios;

- Previous working relationships with vendors and products on the part of your staff (i.e. at their last job they used a particular solution and liked or disliked it);
- A consultant or systems integrator who has relationships with various vendors and/or who has benched staff with particular sets of expertise with different products;
- Staff with a purely functional viewpoint who favor a solution because it works for them whether or not other functional areas are satisfied or not;
- The building of personal relationships with vendor staff during the selection process.

The project team should be made aware of the bias issue and asked to try to make decisions in the light of the project requirements and the enterprise as a whole.

Making the Decision

Based on the RFP responses, interaction with vendors, demonstrations, reference checks and other activities, a decision will need to be made. If a suitable scoring mechanism was devised in conjunction with the RFP then in part, this will be quantitative but it will also be based on the project team's opinions as regards cultural fit, product ease of use and appeal, how well they know the vendor and what they have heard from external colleagues about the vendors, amongst other reasons. For this reason, the decision will most likely be difficult and certainly not entirely clear cut. Additionally, it is likely to be a committee decision (the selection committee) and it will need to weigh the pros and cons, including project costs and timescales, in order to make a decision.

In reality, it is often useful to decide on a solution and a back up and to conduct contract negotiations with both. The reason for this is that the contract negotiation stage can sometimes bring up additional issues that can potentially become showstoppers. By negotiating with two vendors, if one subsequently drops out or proves unable to come to a satisfactory contractual agreement, then the other is still there. If only one winning solution is selected for contract negotiation but the contract cannot be satisfactorily reached, then it is more difficult to go back to other vendors who have already been informed that they were unsuccessful.

CHAPTER 5

THE BEAUTY PAGEANT – SOFTWARE DEMONSTRATIONS

Dr. Gary M. Vasey,

UtiliPoint International, Inc.

The software demonstration can be the ultimate test for both the vendor and the selector but it requires significant preparation on the part of both parties. The overall objective of a software demonstration is to prove that the software is functional, can meet the major requirements of the users and, that is easy and intuitive to use.

Characteristics of ETRM Software impacting the Demonstration

Configurability

Modern ETRM software is extremely configurable and very powerful. While configurability provides the ability for the same software package to have broad applicability across all niches of the industry, it also means that this is complex software that is difficult to learn quickly. Indeed, the software can sometimes be so highly configurable that even many of the vendor's own staffs are not fully aware of its true power and capabilities. During implementation, lack of total familiarity with the software can actually result in unnecessary work arounds being created in some instances! But it also means that a short demonstration can not truly provide anything but a superficial glimpse into the workings of the software and its true capabilities. It is incumbent upon the vendor to ensure that their software demonstration is configured correctly but at the end of the day, they will demonstrate only a subset of functions and features – hopefully the one's that they consider to be competitive differentiators or those that will meet some aspect of your business requirements.

ETRM Software Releases and Upgrades

Before beginning a discussion of demonstrations it is worthwhile considering ETRM software in general from a release and upgrade perspective. A comprehensive ETRM software package is both complex and broad in its functional coverage and the energy industry evolves very rapidly. The vendor is also in the business of selling its software and is therefore constantly adding to its software's features and functionality to meet business changes and to position itself to win new business. This naturally often translates into a hectic release schedule for the software which has implications for those selecting software as well. It is therefore imperative to keep in mind during the selection process and demonstrations that the functionality and features being offered and displayed may not yet be in the released version of the vendor's software.

System Performance

The vendor will likely demonstrate the software on a high end laptop where it may not perform as fast as it would in a run time environment. This should be borne in mind when observing the demonstration. On the other hand, poor performance during the demonstration can point to potential downstream performance issues.

Preparation

The selector should first determine what the objective of the software demonstration is and carefully consider how to organize the demonstrations to meet these goals. With ETRM software, which can be complex, cover a broad range of functionality and features, as well as involve a great deal of configuration, this is extremely important. If proper goals are not set and the vendor is allowed to structure a demonstration then they will do so naturally by showing their strengths and glossing over their weaknesses with a slick demonstration.

One easy way to avoid this is to build scenarios using real data that reflects the actual business that the software will need to support. This is time consuming but well worthwhile since it forces the vendors to come prepared to show exactly how aspects of their software can support the business. However, it also recommended that the vendors are instructed to show how a single deal can be entered and tracked all the way through the system to an invoice since this demonstrates the straight through processing capabilities of the system.

Other areas to consider in planning the demonstrations are reporting and ease of access to the data in the system. By building a set of goals for the demonstrations and providing business scenarios and real data to the vendors you also establish more of a level playing field by which to judge the different systems on display.

Since each vendor has limited time to demonstrate what is in reality, a complex enterprise system, it is also advisable to be disciplined during the demonstrations. This requires the adoption of good meeting practice and rules on the part of the staff attending the demonstration. Lots of *ad hoc* questions during the demonstration can result in an incomplete or hurried presentation which is both unfair to the vendor and results in the selector staff not being given a complete view of the software. Use flipcharts, capture questions and have the vendor respond at the end of the meeting if possible.

In setting goals, it is advisable to consider the following with respect to ETRM software:

- Can the vendor adequately demonstrate straight through processing?
- Does the system have sufficient configurability and flexibility to handle the majority of your business?
- Can the vendor handle the provided business scenarios and data without use of work arounds?
- Does it actually produce the results you expect from the data sets and if not, why not?
- What functionality and features being demonstrated are not yet in the current release and when might they be available?
- Does the system provide easy access to the data that it captures and calculates?
- How paper reports are produced and how easy is it to modify/tailor them?
- How 'easy' is the system to use ad interact with generally?
- How configurable is it and how is the configuration performed? Does it require a super user to set up and maintain configuration?
- How are the software functionality and features presented to the user?
- Ensure that the demonstration calls for an examination of the audit trailing, security and other 'background' functionality.

While impossible to ensure that the demonstration will adequately show that the system can handle all of your business requirements, a well thought through and prepared set of business scenarios can provide some assurances that it will satisfy the majority of the requirements without enhancement.

Finally, it will pay to develop some sort of scoring mechanism or approach by which to judge the vendors and their products. The scoring mechanism can be developed from the objectives devised for the demonstrations and will help remove too much subjectivity from the decision making process.

The Demonstration

The actual demonstration should allow time for the vendor to provide an overview of their company and software product prior to starting the actual software demonstration. As ETRM software is extremely complex and configurable, you will want to understand the architecture of the software and its main functions and features prior to beginning the demonstration. Additionally, the vendor will most likely have pre-configured the software and set it up for use with your business scenarios but it is advisable to have the vendor explain set-up and configuration as a part of the demonstration since this can be quite complex.

The demonstration can also provide you with a feel for the cultural fit between your firm and the supplier. How does the vendor's staff behave? How prepared are they? How do they react to queries and questions? Of course, even the best prepared demonstration can have hitches and issues but fatal errors that occur during the demonstration afford some clues as to the vendor's software's reliability. It is also common practice for the vendor to show various features of the system but never actually save any data. By using actual business scenarios, the vendor will be required to actually hit the save or update button.

For the vendor, the demonstration is a means to display what they have to impress the potential buyer. This means that they should be properly prepared, have the right equipment with them and have presentation materials available to help explain the inner workings and architecture of their proposed solution.

Finally, do bear in mind that the demonstration can only hope to give a feel for the system. ETRM solutions are far too complex to be able to provide a complete demonstration of the system in a small number of hours. By being prepared with goals, objectives and business scenarios however, you can obtain the maximum value from the short demonstration.

Words of caution

The vendor will come to the demonstration with its best and most knowledgeable resources in order to answer your questions, display their expertise and to be able to use their software to its maximum capabilities. The staffs that perform the demonstration may have no role at all in the implementation project and it is advisable to understand that you are seeing the very best the vendor has to offer at this stage. If the vendor is really good in its demonstration approach, they will follow good meeting practice and if questions or issues arise that cannot be addressed during the demonstration they will wish to follow up later.

The vendor will also likely want to display its competitive advantages. Often, this can take the form of showing various features and functions that they believe are their competitive edge and perhaps mentioning potential flaws and weaknesses in likely competitor's products. This may not be done overtly but by having you agree that you would not procure an ETRM solution that could not provide such and such functionality. In fact, the vendor should always be asked what they believe their competitive edge is.

Once again, the vendor is putting on a show for the prospective buyer. In the software business it is quite easy to build things into a demonstration that are actually not a function or feature of the current version of the software. In fact, it is quite common for vendors to demonstrate the very latest version of their software which may actually not yet be available for general release. For this reason, it obviously pays to ask what features and functionality being demonstrated is not yet in the current release and when they will be available. Even then, there are no guarantees that the vendor will actually make the envisaged release dates. It is therefore advisable to insist that the vendor fully discloses *what is certain to be available* at the time of implementation.

In reality, the ETRM solutions being demonstrated will only anyway be a partial fit to your business requirements – perhaps as high as 80-90%. There will be holes or weaknesses in all software products demonstrated and the vendors will almost certainly wish to omit or gloss over this if at all possible during the demonstration. UtiliPoint surveys have indicated that more than 90% of ETRM implementation projects required enhancements to be made to the software as a part of the overall ETRM implementation project and that this activity took up around 26% of the total project effort[2]. Buyers should therefore explicitly ask where the vendor believes their product has shortcomings versus the requirements and how these will be addressed.

The Role of References

Vendor references are important points of comparison and should be approached as a part of the overall procurement project. But why leave it at just vendor provided references? Do some additional research and call other users of the software for their opinion. These reference checks can be used to compare what the consensus view of the vendor's demonstration was versus usage in a real world business. While this is extremely good input it also pays to ask what version of the vendor's software is currently being utilized since the comparison might not hold if there have been major upgrades to the software.

After the Demonstrations

After the demonstrations any follow up items with each vendor should be addressed and the vendors scored according to the objectives and scoring criteria developed for the demonstrations. Make sure that the scoring criteria include some weighting for other observable factors during the demonstration such as degree of vendor preparedness, cultural fit, and industry expertise and so on. In addition to the quantitative scoring, collect subjective comments and opinion from the selection team since this can also be valuable input.

The demonstration scoring and feedback will be considered in conjunction with the RFP responses and other selection activities in

---

[2] Energy Trading, Transaction and Risk Management Software Implementation Projects Snapshot Survey Results, UtiliPoint, 2007

making a final selection. Often, however, it can be advisable to road test the selected software solution using hands on demonstration.

The Road Test

Usually, the demonstration will be entirely conducted by the vendor staff. The will interact with their software and you will observe. While a useful hands-on session can really help in differentiating between solutions but it requires even more staffing and preparation – particularly on the part of the vendor – and the vendor may wish to charge for a hands on session as a result. However, arranging a hands-on session prior to making an ultimate decision can be an extremely useful tactic in the selection process since it allows your users to actually sit behind the system and use it in anger. They can try to break the software and try out certain scenarios that the demonstration did not cover as well as simply get a feel for interacting with the software.

A hands-on session will most likely require a project of its own since the software will need to be installed and generically configured for the process. It will require that the vendor provides a team of staff to support the users adequately, some small amount of training on the system and resources from the selector to use the system. In short, it's an expensive exercise but it can also be the final test before engaging in an even more expensive implementation project.

Again, the hands-on will need careful planning and preparation. Base data will need to be entered, the system configured and business scenarios designed for the users to enter. Expected results will need to be calculated and objectives and goals devised for the sessions. While these are disadvantages in considering a road test the advantages include allowing real users actual interaction with the proposed software, gaining a sense of the vendor's support and training capabilities, the use of more extensive and more complex business scenarios and an idea of how the system and systemized business processes actually perform.

Summary

Demonstrations are an essential component in ETRM software selection but need to be approached with diligence and forward planning. The demonstration needs to be considered as a part of the evaluation process but by their very nature can sometimes become the overall focus for subjective and objective opinion in the selection. For that reason, the selector should be diligent in ensuring that the goals and objectives for the demonstration are understood by the selection team and that they are scored as a part of the overall selection process.

CHAPTER 6

THE NEXT STEP - NEGOTIATION

Dr. Gary M. Vasey,

UtiliPoint International, Inc.

So the software has been selected, the vendor notified and now contracting starts in earnest. The first item on the agenda is the software license agreement. What is it? What does it mean and what are the alternatives? This chapter will review those issues in detail.

Negotiation

Negotiations begin between the buyer and the supplier to actually procure the software. The chances are that there will be at least three, if not four, areas or contracts to negotiate; the software license, the support & maintenance agreement, the services agreement covering the implementation and possibly, a separate software escrow agreement. But this part of the process is also where things can sometimes unexpectedly go wrong as failure to come to acceptable terms over contracts reveals troubling cultural differences between the buyer and the supplier. In reality, at this stage there shouldn't be any surprises. All of these documents should have been provided by the vendor in the RFP or, as a part of the selection process, and costs should already have been quoted and agreed upon by this stage.

Sometimes issues crop up because the project becomes the property of another department; usually purchasing. If the purchasing department isn't familiar with procuring software then there will certainly be issues as the often beaurocratic procurement processes normally used to procure paper clips are used to procure mission critical software. The purchasing department needs to be guided through the process by the actual buyer to help smooth the process along. On the other hand, it can sometimes be the vendor who is unwilling to be flexible. In either case, there is actually a chance that contract negotiations will break down at this stage. That's why it pays to negotiate with two vendors.

The negotiation process really marks the start of a relationship – a partnering relationship between the vendor and the supplier. Both parties should be motivated to achieve a contractual relationship that both protects each company but is overall a win-win scenario. If that's not the case and one side tries to gain an upper hand, it has a very good chance of being the beginning of the end of the relationship.

Traditional Licensing Parameters

Most ETRM software vendors will offer a traditional software licensing arrangement. The license will spell out the terms of usage of the software and offer some warranties regarding its use. It might include a period of free support (usually 90 days), it might not. The license fee will most likely be determined using a price list that has a base fee (perhaps per module to be used) and then additional fees based on the number of named users that will have an account to access the software. In a competitive bidding situation, it's not unusual for the vendor to discount the list price by some percentage. Of course, during negotiations, it is possible to discuss specific pricing terms off of the standard price list and to have those prices held for a specified period of time. In essence, this is a set of negotiated licensing rates specific to your company and the vendor will almost certainly be keen to do this if there is a good chance for your use of the system to grow fairly rapidly in the near future.

The license agreement might call for other fees and payments too. These can include additional fees for multiple installations, multiple entities utilizing the software, fees for additional modules and an escrow fee (if not a separate agreement).

The software license agreement governs the terms of your usage of the software being licensed and it pays to read it carefully.

However, in recent years, new pricing models have emerged in licensing ETRM software and the vendor might be willing to consider other models or indeed actually prefer them. For example, instead of licensing by seats (users – usually in increments of 10 seats or so), licensing might be feasible based on usage as measured by the number of trades entered into the software on a monthly or annual basis. In practice however, vendors prefer a seat basis to licensing because it is simply easier for them to audit. And the vendor will likely have a right to audit your usage of their software built into the license agreement.

Another alternative is to price and license based on simultaneous users. This system provides the user company with a maximum number of concurrent users on the system at any time. On the surface it can appear substantially more expensive but in practice, if the user company has many users who use the software infrequently and just a few who use it all of the time, this could be a more economic option. Essentially, instead of paying a fee for a user (a seat) to use the software once or twice a month, the fee allows only a specified number of (concurrent) users to be using the system at the same time. Of course, the fee for a fixed number of concurrent users will be more substantial than for the same number of seats but more 'seats' than concurrent users will normally be required.

Other Options Emerging

As the ETRM universe matures, other licensing models are emerging. Many of these are described below.

The ASP Solution

The ASP (application service provider) model is exclusively offered by a small number of vendors but almost all vendors will consider it under the right circumstances. In an ASP model, the software is hosted by the vendor or third-party and the users access to it is via the internet or private network. The technology used to provide this service is mature and so security and data mingling are not an issue.

The advantage to an ASP solution is that no installation is required on site and no hardware or support infrastructure is required on the part of the user. For that reason it is both cheaper and less time consuming process to get up and running on the software. Only user training is really required along with some initial configuration. Another advantage of the ASP model is that it is easier to decide to discontinue using the software solution. Other advantages include the fact that software and hardware upgrades will be performed by the vendor or party hosting the software with minimal disruption to the users.

An ASP model will usually be priced as if you were leasing the software. A set number of users will be granted access to the system for a monthly fee.

Where the ASP model has disadvantages is when the required solution is not a plain vanilla version and customization is required. At that point, the economics of the model begin to break down for the vendor since they are in fact hosting a customized solution. For this reason, hosted solutions have been largely the dominion of smaller energy traders who need cheap and secure access to an ETRM solution and do not need much in the way of custom or specialized functionality.

Leasing

Recently, some vendors in the ETRM space have begun to offer leasing options. Essentially this can be a cross between traditional licensing and an ASP model. The software is installed at the user's site but instead of paying license fees the user simply pays a monthly fee for its use.

Other Models

Other models continue to emerge including the use of common code or platforms which are then used to build a custom solution. All that is licensed is the common platform since the customizations are paid for in full and remain the property of the purchaser as opposed to the vendor. Support and maintenance is offered in a completely different manner too in such a scenario.

Enhancements

UtiliPoint research shows that more than 90% of ETRM implementation projects require enhancements to be made to the software. All enhancements should be identified up front and the prices negotiated with the vendor for their development in addition, it pays to negotiate hourly fees for any additional enhancements in advance. You should also specify to the vendor if any of the enhancements are deemed to be proprietary since it is usual practice for the vendor to own the rights to any modifications or enhancements to its software. If something is truly unique, proprietary or sensitive then you should specifically negotiate the rights to that software and expect to pay full fees for its development.

Other Issues to Consider

When licensing software you are essentially simply paying to use it. The software and any enhancements made to it will by default belong to the vendor. For this reason, a buyer can sometimes obtain favorable terms for enhancements by taking the approach that the buyer is providing something that the vendor can package up and continue to sell to other clients. In fact, this will most likely occur anyway but it pays to ask for a discount in return for the expertise needed to develop the enhancement.

When considering license fees, other items can sometimes be negotiated into the agreement in return for discounted fees. These include such things as providing a press announcement for the vendor on successful completion of the implementation, agreeing to be a reference site or agreeing to provide the vendor with a written case study. Today, many buyers are unwilling to endorse their chosen vendor for a variety of reasons and so the vendor will most likely place a value on these things.

It also pays to carefully consider future usage of the software. Will the use of the software grow? Now is the time to negotiate discounted prices for future licensing extensions and by taking some time to think this through, money can be saved in the future.

SECTION 3

IMPLEMENTING YOUR ETRM SYSTEM

INTRODUCTION

Mr. Patrick Reames,

UtiliPoint International, Inc.

Coming out of the system selection process, the buyer is now faced with the task of taking that newly acquired software product and transitioning their data and business process to the new system.

One of the difficulties in writing about ETRM implementations is that there is no "unifying theory" that can be used to fully describe every potential ETRM project. Every project is a unique combination of numerous elements, variables, and expectations.

Vendors

There are literally dozens of vendors of ETRM solutions selling products in North America and around the world. Each vendor has taken a specific, and occasionally unique, approach to addressing the complexities of buying, selling, producing, transporting, and accounting for energy commodities.

The "technology stacks" deployed are unique and for many vendors, are undergoing near constant change and evolution as the technology state of the art continues to advance at breakneck speeds. Java, .Net, n-tier, SOAP, SOA are not just buzz words and acronyms, they are fundamental changes to the technologies that form the core of mission critical systems used by energy commodity trading and marketing organizations. These technologies will impact the ability of a client's organization to install, configure, maintain, and interface to their selected ETRM solution.

The deployment of ASP delivered ETRM software is becoming more commonplace. The differences between these ASP solutions and the traditionally delivered solutions go beyond just the location of the server. ASP solutions currently serve a very well defined market and generally provide limited commodity coverage. However, for the markets that they do serve, they have been very successful. If a company has selected an ASP delivered solution, the implication would be that their business models are a good fit for the specific functional and commodity coverage offered by that product.

Commodity coverage varies by vendor, and the depth of functionality provided around that commodity will also vary. For example: a vendor advertising the ability to manage power trading in their system will, of course, be telling the truth. However, what aspects of power trading are included in their coverage? Can the system facilitate real-time trading/scheduling? Can it communicate with the ISO/RTO's for scheduling? Does it do NERC tagging? Is it compliant with the new California MRTU or the Texas Nodal market? Clearly, coming out of the product selection process you have to know the products capabilities and plan accordingly.

The nature (physical or financial) of the commodities traded will also have a significant impact on the types of activities and efforts expended during the implementation. Financial only implementations will be significantly narrower in scope and shorter in duration that one that involves the management of physical commodities.

Vendors will also differ in their ability to support a client in the implementation process. Many vendors have built large service organizations that are focused on providing deep business knowledge and advanced technical and project management skills. Others have chosen to focus their organizations around product development only and have established relationships with third party consulting companies for services coverage for their clients.

Clients

Customers that purchase an ETRM system vary from a 3 man shop trading financial commodities, to multinational companies, producing, trading, marketing and moving multiple physical commodities and hedging those commodities in financial markets around the world. Clearly a "one size fits all" implementation process is out of the question.

Variables impacting the implementation process for a customer will include: user counts, number/nature/volumes of traded commodities, geographic scope, organizational structure, business processes, executive philosophies, regulatory exposures, strategy, assets, and the list goes on and on.

Clearly, it is not possible to create an implementation road map that addresses every possible permutation of all these elements. What is possible, however, is to provide some generalized views of the activities that must take place and some "rules of the road" that have been derived from the experiences of the product vendors, service companies, and clients that have been down the implementation path many times since FERC 636.

High Cost, High Risk Projects

Few implementation projects have failed because the software didn't function. In fact, it would be difficult to legitimately point to a single packaged ETRM software implementation project in the last 5 years that was considered a failure because the software was not functional. That's not to say that there have not been failures. There have, in fact, been quite a few. First of all, let's define failure. On one extreme, there is a "complete failure", meaning the software was not fully implemented and is completely unusable for its intended purpose. On the other extreme is a "partial failure", meaning the software was implemented; however, it failed, for whatever reason, to meet the expectations that the client had for it when it was purchased. A true complete failure is rare. In fact, a recent UtiliPoint study indicated that of 35 ETRM projects surveyed, only one could be said to be a complete failure, never having actually gone "live". However, of the 35 projects, more than 25% indicated that their projects were not implemented properly – these would be the partial failures, projects that did not live up to their expectations.

A 25% failure rate is alarming. Consider the time and dollars expended to acquire and implement an ETRM product: UtiliPoint's data indicates an "average" implementation will require 9 months to a year to implement, and the median initial licensing cost will be well over $500,000, with total implementation costs averaging 1.5 to 2.5 times the license cost. Obviously implementations are high cost/high risk projects.

What's Next

Again, acknowledging the uniqueness of every client and every project, in this section we will examine the implementation process, focusing particular attention on implementation methodologies, implementation team structuring, key success factors, the use of consultants in the process, and an in-depth look at the process of testing throughout the implementation.

ETRM Implementation "Golden Rules"

1. Choose the right product
2. Define success
3. Be a partner with your vendor
4. Own the Project
5. Employ skilled Project management
6. Dedicate personnel to the Project
7. Incentivize and celebrate Success
8. Maintain Momentum
9. Emphasize Training
10. Test, test, and test

CHAPTER 7

IMPLEMENTING ETRM SOFTWARE –
A BENCHMARK STUDY

Dr. Gary M. Vasey

&

Mr. Patrick Reames,

UtiliPoint International, Inc.

In anticipation of preparing this book, UtiliPoint conducted an electronic survey into the implementation of Energy Trading, Transaction and Risk Management (ETRM) software (UtiliPoint International, Inc., 2007) obtaining a total of 35 responses during the period of March and April, 2007. The survey was conducted as a 'snapshot' survey using an internet-based survey instrument only and targeting various email lists maintained by UtiliPoint. This chapter outlines the survey's results and our analysis.

The respondents to the survey represented a good geographic range of project experience with respondents from North American, European and Asian implementation projects. They represented a diverse range of software vendors and products, including custom solutions. They also included a number of consulting companies that undertake ETRM software implementations.

Survey Results

The average duration ETRM project takes 11-months and has an average cost of around twice the initial license fee.

There were no obvious relationships between project duration and the product that was being implemented, or, between project duration and project activities such as data conversion or integration. As a generalization, there was a suggestion in the data, as well might be expected, that more complex projects lasted longer; so for example, it generally takes longer to implement a complete ETRM product such as Allegro, ZaiNet or OpenLink than it does to implement a component of ETRM such as @Energy from FEA or nMarket from the Structure Group. But this is not true in every case according to the data! Another generalization that can be made is that companies with a more asset-heavy business tend to take longer to implement ETRM software. Again, this would be an obvious conclusion without the survey data since their business is potentially significantly more complex than a financial energy trader.

Just under half of the respondents said that their implementation costs were either the same or less than the software license fee that they paid, on the other hand, more than a quarter of the respondents said that their ETRM implementation had cost them three or more than three times the license fee (Figure 1). Again, there were no obvious correlations apparent in the data between the cost of the implementation project and other factors save those generalizations mentioned in the section above on project duration.

Figure 1: Cost of ETRM Implementation Projects

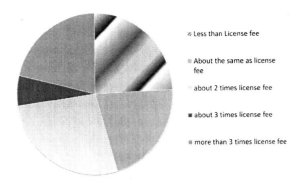

- Less than License fee
- About the same as license fee
- about 2 times license fee
- about 3 times license fee
- more than 3 times license fee

The survey also asked respondents to estimate the percentage of project time spent on several important implementation activities. These included historical data conversion, integration activities, training and enhancements to the product. Activities such as data conversion and integration can add substantially to project cost and complexity in our experience.

Almost all respondents undertook user training and, on average, spent about 10% of their total project engaged in this activity. Interestingly, about 93% of the respondents reported that enhancements were made to their software as a part of the overall ETRM implementation project and that this activity took up around 26% of the total project effort. Integration activities impacted around 90% of all respondent's ETRM implementation projects and this activity expended on average 22% of project time. Lastly, historical data conversion was undertaken by 73% of the respondent's projects and used a further 12% of project effort on average.

It is potentially surprising that so many ETRM implementations involve significant enhancements but UtiliPoint has previously observed that vendor-provided ETRM solutions are often no more than a 70-80% fit to a specific user's requirements (Vasey & Bruce, 2006) simply due to the complexity of the industry and its different business models at a detailed level. The current survey data appears to confim that fact and certainly suggests that buyers should anticipate the need to make enhancements to vendor-provided software at some level.

Historical data converson can have a significant impact on an implementation project depending upon implementation choices around whether or not to convert historical data and if so, how much history to convert. The primary considerations when undertaking data conversion is the quality, source(s), and nature of that historical data. Often, historical data as been maintained in multiple systems and is of suspect quality making a data cleansing step a necessity in the implementation project potentially adding to the complexity and cost of that project. The nature of the data, that is "static" or "transactional", will probably be the largest determinate of effort/cost of any conversion effort.

Data reflecting the actual transactions (that is a "deal" comprised of a point, volume, price, and term) will vary in its representation from system to system. Attempting to convert this level of data can be very problematic and, in many cases, virtually impossible. Static data, that is data and information that is rarely changing (such as pipeline, points, counterparty information) is a much more viable candidate for programatic extranction and conversion.

A favored approach to dealing with the issue of maintaining historical transactional data is to retain the legacy systems for historical reporting, reconciliation, and audit purposes, thus making a fresh start with the new software which will reflect transactions effective with the "cut-over" date. But, this approach does have its drawbacks as it requires those legacy systems to be maintained for some period of several years into the future.

The survey suggests that the majority of companies surveyed chose to convert at least some historical data, but possibly limited that conversion to "static" data.

Integration is the largest issue facing ETRM software users not just between various modules/components of the chosen solution but also with other corporate systems and even, in some instances, beyond the

74

enterprise itself. As a result, it is no surprise to see that 9 out of 10 respondents undertook integration work and that this aspect of the project was quite substantial in terms of overall project effort.

Figure 2: Project Activities

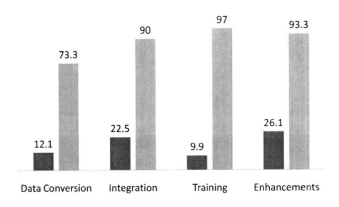

The range of values reported as being spent on each activity was also quite variable as shown in Figure 3. However, as reported above, there was little correlation between the amount of project time spent on these particular activities and the total project duration and/or cost implicit in the survey data. However, integration and enhancement activities are by far the most time consuming.

Figure 3: Project Time and Activities

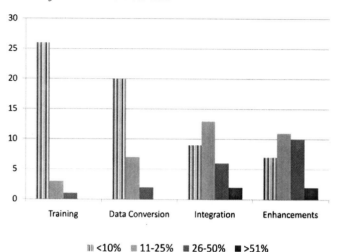

‖ <10%   ▩ 11-25%   ▪ 26-50%   ▪ >51%

Use of Third Party Consultants and Integrators

Many ETRM projects utilize outside assistance in the form of third party consultants (that is resources supplied by companies other than the vendor or client). In the survey, about 30% of the ETRM implementation projects reflected in our survey did not use third party consultants for any purpose whatsoever. Of the other 70% of respondents, third party consultants were mostly used in the role of project managers/office, followed by business process consulting, systems integration consulting, making enhancements and selection consulting.

The survey data then suggests that consultants are more likely to be used on longer and more complex ETRM implementation projects. Again, as previously noted, these third party consultants are most commonly involved in projects involving complete ETRM implementations as opposed to ETRM components, such as risk management tools.

Implementation Experience

ETRM implementation projects have gained a reputation over the years for potentially being very difficult and in some instance, perhaps 'career limiting'.

Our survey suggests however that, on average ETRM projects are not such a bad experience for those involved with them. More than three quarters of the respondents portrayed their experiences as average or better (Figure 5). However, the risks of undertaking an ETRM implementation project are perhaps accurately reflected in the just less than 25% of respondents who said that their experience was poor or even terrible! The survey included one respondent whose project never finished and was abandoned representing a 3% failure rate which is quite low for large and complex IT projects but two other respondents reported their projects to be 'disastrous' representing a 9% failure rate.

Aside from their experiences with the ETRM implementation project, the acid test of success or failure is whether the software is deemed to be properly implemented and our survey shows that in 27% of the projects reported on, the result was that the software was not properly implemented (Figure 6).

Figure 5: ETRM Implementation Project Experience

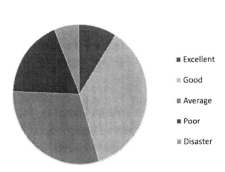

Implementation Experience

- Excellent
- Good
- Average
- Poor
- Disaster

Figure 6: Project Success Rates

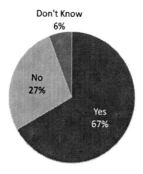

The respondents also provided information in the form of comments about their overall project experience. For those with not such a good experience the largest criticism on the part of the respondents is targeted squarely at the vendor citing issues such as lack of product knowledge among vendor staff, underestimation of project complexity, lack of stated and expected functionality within the product and, poor guidance on system set up and operation. Other common issues included;

- Integration issues;
- Underestimation of time required to complete the project;
- The need for better requirements gathering upfront; and,
- The fact that key staff on the project also still had full-time jobs in the company.

Interestingly, a small number of respondents also said that the software, although properly implemented, was not being utilized to its full capacity by the company.

The comments by the respondents held no surprises. With the growth rates experienced by many of the vendors over recent years many of their staff is relatively new and inexperienced with the vendor's product. In fact, this is not a new criticism of vendors but it is one that should be noted by, and anticipated, by potential buyers. One danger in this trend is that inexperienced vendor staff can result in work arounds being created for particular business scenarios where no such work around is actually required. Much of the ETRM software on the market today is very configurable and highly complex meaning that it simply takes time for users to fully appreciate its power – including vendor project implementation staff.

Another key comment targeted at vendors was lack of promised functionality. The ETRM software market is both rapidly moving in terms of requirements and also very competitive which has resulted in a tendency to 'oversell' or prematurely sell product features and functions. Another potential explanation for this particular issue is a misunderstanding of the client's requirements versus the supplied functionality. Energy trading is certainly one of the more challenging business processes to model. The complexity of the business, coupled with unique or proprietary business processes within the market participants can lead to misunderstanding as to business requirements. In UtiliPoint's experience, it is not uncommon for misunderstanding in relation to terminology or process to occur. However, this issue also suggests inadequate focus on software selection by the company purchasing and implementing the software since the testing and examination of key features or functionality should have been a primary focus in the selection process. In essence, the blame for this issue lies with the buyer who didn't do a comprehensive check of the vendor claims.

The most important observation among the respondents in our opinion is that user resources on the project were insufficient and/or were still responsible for other full-time jobs at the company. An ETRM implementation project is always likely to be a complex and risky process, requiring the full-time attention of expert staff and resources at the company undertaking the implementation. ETRM is a critical system and its implementation should be a priority of senior management for the project to succeed. For UtiliPoint, it is the comment on the part of the respondents that project staff is not allocated full-time to the project that is among the most worrying. To make that point more clearly, those respondents that felt they had achieved a good, successful implementation often cited good upfront planning, management commitment and strong project management as strongly contributing to their success.

In terms of what respondents would do differently the next time around, their suggestions all fell within the same areas and included;

1. More experienced *and dedicated* staff on the project team with clear and accountable roles and responsibilities; including a dedicated project manager;
2. Allow more time for testing perhaps even piloting the product initially and the use of more detailed test scripts;
3. Spending more time on requirements definition with more focus on just the important functionality that is required to support the business. Ensuring that the product design more closely matches internal business processes;
4. Obtaining clearer specifications from the vendor and being more rigorous in vendor selection in the first place;
5. Ensuring that the vendor implementation team has more depth of experience;
6. Allowing more time to complete the project;

The ingredients to a successful ETRM implementation project are many but in our experience, the biggest difference to the outcome is dictated by the following;

1. Management commitment to the project and its successful outcome reflected in making the necessary budget, resources and expertise available to the project and in communicating the objectives of the project ad management's commitment to it;
2. Proper project planning and resourcing of the project from the company, the vendor and the consultant (if used). Project resources should be full-time where possible or at least not have other over-riding priorities that cause conflict. Roles and responsibilities should be clear and understood;
3. Strong project management is key to a project's success and that project manager should have the authority necessary to

ensure timely decisions are made during the course of the project;

4. Properly understood and documented requirements that take into consideration the environment in which the system will be implemented (i.e. interfaces) and where possible adopt vendor-provided software business processes to avoid work arounds and enhancements;

5. A comprehensive testing strategy that includes real-world testing scenarios, adequate time to fix issues and retest, and a proper testing environment; and finally,

6. Selecting the right vendor and package in the first place.

Summary

As is probably not unexpected, attempting to "boil down" implementation projects to a few key indicators is at best a difficult project. Given the breadth and depth of the various market participants and vendors serving the energy marketing space, it is apparent that there is no "one size fits all" product or implementation project.

However, based upon the survey results, coupled with UtiliPoint's experience and analysis of the space, there are some significant conclusions that can be drawn.

1. The same product deployed at different companies will not take the same amount of time/effort to implement. The variables involved here include:

    a. Complexity of the business model
        i. Number/types of commodities traded
        ii. Physical vs. Financial oriented trading
        iii. Asset heavy vs. asset light business
        iv. Geographic scope of the business
        v. Number of pipelines and/or RTO's/ISO's involved
        vi. Number/type of transportation agreements
        vii. Number of daily transactions
    b. Organizational structure of the company

     i.   Number of Traders

     ii.   Number/Type of Trading Desks

     iii.   Number of schedulers

     iv.   Number of Accountants

     v.   Role of Contract Administration

   c.   Project Structuring

     i.   Dedication and skill level of Client team members

     ii.   Level of involvement of Vendor resources

     iii.   Level of involvement of third party consultants

     iv.   Methodologies utilized

     v.   Training approach

     vi.   Project Management skills

   d.   Other Factors

     i.   Necessity of enhancements

     ii.   Reports development

     iii.   Interfaces/Integration development

     iv.   Nature and scope of data conversion

2.   Conversely, any individual company's time/effort to implement a new ETRM system will be significantly impacted by their selection of a product:

   a.   Many products on the market require "scripting", that is, they require significant "customization" during the implementation process.

   b.   Some products can be implemented "out of the box" and may require little or no customization of code prior to use depending on the customer's business model.

   c.   Reporting capabilities can vary significantly by product

   d.   The method and/or ability to interface/integrate will vary significantly by product

   e.   The "ease of use" will vary by product, impacting training and ultimately user acceptance.

Ultimately, the final determinate of success for any ETRM product implementation is an affirmative response to the question, "Did the product and the process meet my expectations?" Knowing your requirements, finding a product that meets those requirements and understanding the effort necessary to implement that product ultimately will determine whether you and your company will be successful with the acquisition and implementation of any ETRM product.

References

UtiliPoint International, Inc. (2007). *ETRM Software Implementation Projects - Snapshot Survey Results.*

UtiliPoint International, Inc. (2007). *Benchmarking of European ETRM Software Markets.*

UtiliPoint International, Inc. (2006). *ETRM Vendor Perception Study – North America.*

Vasey, G. & Bruce, A. (2006). *Trends in Energy Trading , Transaction and Risk Management Software - A Primer.* Houston: BookSurge Publishing.

CHAPTER 8

THE IMPLEMENTATION PROCESS

Mr. Patrick Reames,

UtiliPoint International, Inc.

An ETRM implementation project is the structured process of taking a newly acquired ETRM software product from delivery of code to full "in production" use, and in the process, meeting the business needs that precipitated its purchase.

In many ways, implementing an ETRM system is much like implementing any other enterprise scale IT systems. It requires a comprehensive plan, solid leadership (both executive and project management), and both technical and business expertise. However, ETRM systems are unique in that they operate as not only the system of record (that is the system that records, maintains, and accounts for transactions), but they also provide tools for managing contracts, deals, logistics, position management, risk management, and associated analytics. ETRM systems are uniquely constructed to be a singular system providing the entire breath of functionality required by energy trading organizations. As such, they are extremely complex systems and require deep functional business knowledge to properly implement.

Scope and Scale

As previously noted in this book, every client, every vendor, and every product is unique. The combinations of variables such as customer expectations, trading activities, assets, staff; product scope, features, technical architecture; and vendor capabilities will create wide variations in required specific activities that will determine the scope and scale of the implementation process for any particular customer. There truly is **no** "one size fits all" granular methodology for implementing a new ETRM system.

In my experience, I have seen project teams comprised of one or two individuals be successful, implementing an ETRM system within a very small trading shop with a limited business scope (single commodity, small geographic reach, limited assets, etc) and a small number of transactions. On the other end of the scale, I've seen project teams comprised of literally hundreds, deploying an ETRM system worldwide, fully integrated into the company's global IT infrastructure and capturing the entirety of their multi-commodity energy trading activities. Obviously, there is not a single detailed model that can be stretched to address the needs of these two groups.

What we will explore in this chapter is a generalized discussion of the common tasks and activities associated with implementing an ETRM system. Depending on where your company lies within the continuum of scale from the very small shop to the one that competes in the global energy markets, your project must scale to meet your needs.

How Long Does It Take to Implement?

As a leader of several different implementation services group, one of the most frustrating questions I had to face day in and day out was being asked by the sales representative, "How long will it take to implement the system for Prospect X (a prospect that I had never heard of)?" The only reasonable answer to that question, without knowing the requisite details associated with that prospective customer was "if everything goes right, somewhere between 3 months and 2 years." Obviously not the answer the sales rep wanted to hear. However, that question "how long will it take" is akin to asking "how long is a string". Without a thorough examination of the variables involved, any estimate is a meaningless number. These variables that will impact the time required include:

1) Product implemented and its "fitness"
   a. Necessity for customization
   b. Necessity for "configuration"
2) Nature of the business implementing
   a. Asset Heavy
   b. Asset Light
3) User counts and skill level
4) Number and time dedication of implementation team members
5) Transaction counts
6) Business processes
7) Organizational structure (functional groups)
8) Client expectations and definition of success
9) Legacy system being replaced
10) Interfacing requirements

Looking at it from a specific customer perspective, most of the leading ETRM products on the market, if taken "straight out of the box" and holding all other variables constant, will require about the same amount of time to implement (plus or minus 10 – 20% depending on the skills of the vendor's implementation teams). The exceptions are those products that require programmatic configuration (scripting). These products, given their customizable nature, may require significantly more time to implement as the process mapping, design, development and testing of the scripts will entail significantly more effort and testing cycles.

Packaged Software vs. Customizable or Hybrid Software

For purposes of this discussion, we will focus on implementing standardized or packaged software; the most common form of ETRM solutions. However, there are other options available in the market and it is important to understand the implications of deploying systems other than those that are pre-packaged and ready to use "out of the box".

A few ETRM systems available on the market offer the ability for the client to "customize" the system through scripting or other such devices. These scripts are utilized to configure screens (adding, removing or relocating information or input fields) and define processes, both in terms of how the system operates and in terms of how you navigate the system.

In many ways, the process of scripting the hybrid or configurable system is akin to a development process. The desired functionally must be defined based on the customers unique requirements – what do they do that may be different from their competitors in the market.

Implementing a hybrid system will, in most cases, increase the customer's reliance on the vendor during the implementation process. While the skills necessary to write the scripts is not particularly unique to the vendor, knowledge of how to effectively translate business processes and procedures to screen layouts and process flows within the systems does require knowledge that will generally lay only with those that are experienced in these types of implementations and the specific product being implemented.

Proprietary Methodologies

Virtually every ETRM vendor and third party consulting organization will advertise a proprietary implementation methodology. Most of these methodologies stress a structured iterative process of data loading, scenario (business case) testing, and adjustment. Each vendor and/or consulting company will bring with them a raft of documentation outlining process and procedures, and providing templates for project management and organization, change management, data cleansing and loading, and product training.

At their core, there is much more in common amongst these various methodologies than differences. Virtually any "road tested" methodology will prove successful if it is properly deployed and managed to. Stated another way, the secret to success for any implementation is to have a solid plan, a good team, executive backing and professional project management that keeps all the pieces moving in concert.

All methodologies share common activity streams and components; however, they may differ in terminology and order of activity. Common to all methodologies are activities that focus on properly initiating the project, developing a project plan, and executing the specific activities required to move the system into full in-production use.

A Common View

To reiterate...our goal with this section is not to give a detailed roadmap for executing an implementation project. Rather we want to try to give a broad overview of many of the activities and discuss some of the potential landmines of implementations. As stated many times before, ETRM system implementations are very complex, with many "moving parts" and dependences amongst the various tasks and deliverables. And again, many vendors or service firms will come with structured "proprietary" methodologies, all of which will have strengths relative to a particular type of customer or product. Again, however, there is no "one size fits all" methodology which can address every customer need or product. There are some very good frameworks for implementing systems, but every one of these needs to be tailored to the particular company and situation in which the product is being deployed. So, with that out of the way, we will note that the implementation of an ETRM system can be distilled to groupings of common activities.

Every implementation is, of course, preceded by the realization that your organization needs a new system. Once that need is acknowledged and accepted by those with the authority to purchase a new system, the process of identifying specific requirements can begin, or as shown in Figure 1 on the following page, the Needs Assessment and Identification. Once the organization has come to a consensus regarding expectations for the new system, the process of reviewing, selecting and acquiring that system can begin (see Chapters 4, 5, and 6 for a detailed discussion of these activities), again referring to Figure 1, this the Solution Selection and Acquisition Phase.

Figure 1

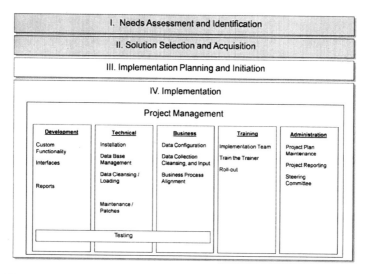

Note: our discussion will exclude the grayed out areas, Phase I. Needs Assessment and Identification and Phase II. Solution Selection and Acquisition, as these are pre-implementation activities and are covered in other chapters of this book (See chapters 4, 5, and 6).

When the contracting for the new system is complete, the hard work begins – the actual implementation activities. For purposes of our discussion, again we'll use Figure 1 as a view of the most common activities and processes involved in an implementation. It is not intended to be an endorsement or advocacy of any particular methodology.

ETRM implementations can be broken down into 5 distinct streams of activities, each defined by the assigned resources: Technical, Business, Development, Training, and Administration. Its important to note that, despite the graphical representation of discreet activities, each of these 5 streams are interconnected and interdependent, with the success of each dependent upon each other, and each forming some part of the overall critical path. The real differentiator between the streams is the types of skills required to complete each.

Implementation Initiation and Planning

Immediately following the selection and contracting (or if practical, prior to the final contracting) of a new ETRM system, the implementation begins.

The first group of activities undertaken post contracting is the project initiation and planning stage. It's during this stage that all the project team members are brought together with the business unit leaders, vendor consultants, executive sponsors, and outside consultants to get the project rolling in the right direction. Depending on the organization size and project/application scope, this phase, which is ultimately a series of meetings, can last from one day to several weeks, not including the preparation of the project plan and associated documentation.

Project initiation should be focused on bringing everyone involved in the project together in one place with the goals of 1) setting expectations, 2) establishing project priorities, and 3) familiarizing the outside members of the team with the scope of the customer's business. Participants should include:

- the executive sponsor,
- the project manager,
- implementation team members,
- heads of affected departments,

- third party integrators, and
- vendor consultants.

A focus for these meetings should be a review of current business processes, familiarizing the entire team with the business activities and processes of the company. This review will identify potentially difficult or problematic issues early in the process and assist in the project plan preparation. Additionally, the project initiation meeting should cover project administration/governance procedures (including status reporting, reporting chain, project calendar, steering committee information, etc.) and establish roles and responsibilities with particular attention given to the roles and responsibilities of the third party consulting resources.

The project initiation meetings also provide an invaluable forum for the project's executive sponsor to clearly state the project's importance to the organization. Ideally, the sponsor will be able to elaborate unqualified support to ensuring the project's success, including rapid issue resolution and willingness to make organizational adjustments as necessary.

The project manager, working in coordination with the vendor's project lead should develop the project plan in MS Project (or similar Gantt Charting tool). The project should be a detailed roadmap of the activities of the project, with all tasks listed and resourced, and the project's critical path identified. The vendor's project manager/lead should be able to provide a template for the Gantt chart based upon their previous experience in implementing their products. Each vendor will have unique activities that are specific to their products and therefore, these will need to be reflected in the project plan.

While many methodologies do not necessarily include one, we would recommend the development of a "project execution plan" (PEP) which is a verbalization of the project plan milestones and deliverables; and includes a comprehensive outline of project governance and procedures. We recommend this for several reasons: 1) not everyone can comprehend a complex Gantt chart, 2) the PEP serves to clearly lay out expectations as to who is responsible for what and at what time, and 3) it serves a place to reaffirm the project goals and expectations, helping to reduce misunderstanding and potential conflict. The PEP should be part and parcel to the Project Plan and should be updated and maintained in parallel to that plan.

Project Activity Streams

Again, referencing Figure 1, we've broken the implementation project down into five distinct activity streams: 1) Development, 2) Technical, 3) Business, 4) Training and 5) Project Administration. In this discussion we've incorporated testing as a component within the project streams. However, if your project is of sufficient scope and scale, it would be advisable to break testing into a separate project stream. For a complete discussion of developing the appropriate testing strategy for your project, see *Chapter 12, The Importance of Testing*.

- **Project Administration**

   The project manager, as noted above, is responsible for coordinating all project activities and managing the implementation staff toward a successful project. The project administration activities include managing, monitoring, coordinating and updating the project plan. Additional key activities involve progress reporting to not only the project steering committee, but also to the users that will be taking up the new system at the end of the project.

   An important element in project administration is change control. Change control is basically the mechanism that keeps the project on track, ensuring that any deviation from the initial plan is thoroughly examined and justified (both in terms of cost and impact) prior to its being adopted and incorporated into the project. Developing appropriate change controls procedures is an important component of project management and will help ensure that the project is completed in a timely fashion.

- **Training Activities**

93

Effective training is a most important activity undertaken during any product implementation. All leading ETRM vendors have established training programs, delivered either by a professional training staff or by their consulting personnel. These training programs generally include formalized classroom materials such as user manuals, training guides, and testing materials.

Training programs should be structured to address the needs of the various participants involved in both the implementation and ongoing use of the system. This includes implementation team training, user training, technical training, and administrator training. Some vendors also offer a "super user" course. Training is generally structured by business module, with specific courses for scheduling, trading, accounting, risk management, and system administration; and technical courses such as report writing, database administration, and interface development.

o **Implementation Team Training** - Without a thorough understanding of system capabilities, requirements, and navigation, the implementation team cannot make the informed decisions that must be made during the implementation process, leading to a poorly or incorrectly implemented system. Training of implementation team members should focus not only on their specific area of responsibility, but should also include training on the functions immediately upstream and downstream of their immediate area, as implementation decisions made by one group will impact the groups surrounding them. Training for the implementation team should involve in-depth instruction on all functions and processes of the system so as to ensure the team understands all the system's capabilities. Once the team fully understands the "ins and outs" of the system, including the different process options available to them, they should spend time inputting and testing actual business scenarios that reflect the day to day business of the customer. It's during this training that the team can first start to formulate the mapping of their business processes against the system's functionality.

- o **User Training** - The non-implementation team users of the system must be fully trained in the use of the system and their responsibilities to it prior to the system going into production. Experience warns us that without adequate training, user dissatisfaction with the system can increase to the point that the new system ultimately fails. User training will be a combination of instruction on the functionality of the system and the specific business processes used by the customer. Ideally, non-implementation team users should be trained just prior to entering into parallel usage.

- o **Super User Training** - Every organization should have at least two super users, individuals that are fully trained in all aspects of the systems and who fully understand how the system is used within the organization. Generally, super users should be implementation team members and should receive training on all aspects of the system, not just the areas that are part of their day to day user responsibilities.

- **Development Activities**

The development activity stream may or may not be required depending on the "fitness" of the application. In many cases the product will be deployed and implemented "as is", meaning that no changes or additions are required. However, it is not unusual for a customer to require additional functionality to cover unique business activities or processes not adequately addressed in the product. This is particularly true for reports and interfaces.

- o **Reports** – When ETRM systems first become commercially available in the early to mid 90's, reporting was considered to be a major shortcoming for virtually every system on the market. The vendors attempted to remedy this by working with their clients to take customer developed reports, bring them into the supported product stream and package them for sale to new and existing customers. Unfortunately, this lead to libraries of supplied reports that could number in the hundreds with few applicable to any single customer. Fortunately, the major ETRM vendors have moved away from the model of trying to anticipate every clients needs, and have instead packaged powerful ad hoc reporting tools with their systems. These tools are capable of allowing novice users to define custom reports through a menu driven interface. They can save the report and rerun it as they desire. With these new reporting tools, any reports requested by users during the implementation should be reviewed in terms of what can be achieved through these reporting tools.

o **Interfaces** – This is also an area that has come a long way since ETRM systems were first available. The advent of java based integration points and messaging systems has allowed vendors to move past cumbersome file transfers in order to move data into and out of their systems. In fact, most vendors now support interfaces to the most commonly used applications ancillary to the ETRM systems, including the Intercontinental Exchange (ICE), Platts price feeds, SAP, and other ERP and accounting systems. As such, for the technical resources involved in the project, interfacing to and from the ETRM system is more akin to technical "plumbing" as opposed to create complicated ETL (extract, transform, and load) interfaces.

Due to the highly variable nature of projects involving the development of custom ETRM functionality (scope, complexity, technology), we will not discuss development methodologies in this article. For more information on managing and implementing development programs, we would suggest consulting one of the many excellent texts that have been written on the. It should be noted however, that if a company is pursuing the development of additional features or functionality, that development effort must be accounted for in the project plan and must be part and parcel to the overall implementation. Newly developed features and functions must be completed, unit tested, and integrated into the overall technical and business infrastructure of the project.

- **Technical Activities**

  As part of the project initiation process, the technical team from the product vendor or the implementation team, should undertake a comprehensive review of the customer's technical infrastructure (that is server availability and capacities, network configuration and desktop machines) in order to confirm that the customer has properly configured the environment in alignment with the new products requirements. The customer should have, prior to the project initiation phase, reviewed the selected vendor's technical infrastructure requirements in order to ensure that they had adequate resources in place prior to undertaking any activities.

  o **Product Installation** - The technical team, comprised of appropriately skilled technical resources from both the vendor and the customer, will undertake the actual installation of the product(s). This will include installing the executable code on the appropriate server(s), deploying any code necessary to the users' desktops, installing/configuring the database(s) and establishing and testing communication amongst the various elements. Once the system is fully installed, it should be tested by the vendor to ensure that all components are fully installed and functioning as intended.

  o **Integration** – Establishing communication from the ETRM system to related systems in order to exchange data/information. Systems commonly integrated to the ETRM system include price feeds, ICE exchange information, accounting/ERP systems, RTO interfaces, and other logistics systems. Historically, these integration activities have involved setting up data file transfers; however, today many of these integration points involve transferring data via web services and XML.

- o **Report Development** – As recently as a couple of years ago, much time and effort were spent by the technical implementation team developing custom reports. However, a growing trend has been for ETRM vendors to equip their systems with more powerful ad-hoc report writing capabilities, helping to relieve some of the burden from the technical team. Still, most implementations will still require some level of report development by the implementation team, especially those reports that require data to be consolidated across multiple systems.

- **Business Activities**

The business implementation activities involve data configuration, modeling, testing, and establishing processes associated with use of the newly installed system.

- o **Defining System Required Data Elements** – Every ETRM system will require the establishment of certain data elements or fields. These will include defining deal types (spot, firm, etc), contract types (bilateral, sales, purchase, etc.), counter party types, contact types, etc. Ultimately, the definition of these elements will depend on the terminology used and processes employed by the customer. These elements are the lowest level of the data hierarchy, and as such, it is of the utmost importance to get them right prior to using the system in production. Few if any ETRM products allow users to change these elements once they are used. For instance if you establish a deal type as "spot" and you use that deal type to record a transaction, you cannot globally change "spot" to "short-term"; it would have to be done at the individual transaction level. It's very important to make sure these elements are thoroughly considered prior to committing them to the system.

o **Data collection** – The business implementation team will be responsible for data collection and cleansing. The team will gather all the counter party contracts, including marketing agreements, services agreements, location information (pipeline, grid, points, meters, etc), and accounting data (general ledger accounts, etc). The sources for this data will of course vary by customer and will depend upon the various "systems of record" previously in use. These systems could be anything from previously deployed ETRM systems to paper based records.

o **Data Cleansing** – Once the data is collected and collated, the team needs to ensure that it is accurate and up to date.

o **Data Loading** – Data can be loaded into the new system via two methods – programmatically or via manual entry. The decision to use either method will depend on a number of factors, including source/nature (hardcopy or electronic) of the data, the volume of data (number of contracts, number of transaction points, etc) and the skills and availability of resources. Once loaded, the data needs to be reviewed for accuracy and completeness.

o **Scenario Testing** – *Note: See Chapter 12 for a comprehensive discussion of testing strategies.* Post training, the implementation team should be adequately armed to start making preliminary decisions as to how they will use the system. These preliminary decisions should be documented and tested immediately following the initial data loading. This testing should include both existing transactions and potential new "deals". Additionally, the testing should simulate a complete business cycle; that is, taking deals from the inception of a business month, adding incremental transactions, and carrying all through an accounting close. The testing should focus on only on the capture of data, but the process "hand-offs" that will occur during live use. Once the scenarios have been input and processed, all the system products (reports, statements, accounting entries, etc) should be reviewed for correctness and completeness.

o **Business Process Alignment** – *Not be confused with Business Process Re-engineering.* Business Process Alignment is best described as matching your business process to your new ETRM system and vice versa. It is an exercise that involves the disciplines of "Change Management", and it is recommended that any organization that is undergoing significant changes to their internal processes embrace a comprehensive change management program to better facilitate those changes. If you do not have the expertise internally to execute such a program, it is recommended that you seek outside help in ensuring your organization is properly aligned with and accepting of the changes that may occur with the implementation of a new ETRM system.

As noted above, scenario testing involves not only testing the data load and data configuration, it's also the time to begin formulating the necessary processes and handoff changes that will be required with any new system. While virtually every system on the market will attempt to mirror the common business practices associated with the various commodities they handle, each of those systems will have unique requirements in terms of how data is captured and moved from one area of responsibility to another. Coming out of training the implementation team members should have a fair understanding of the process implications of the new system. Using this preliminary understanding, the team should undertake to define roles and responsibilities associated with the specific data handling requirements of the system, such as:

✓ What person/role should be responsible for inputting new contracts or enabling agreements?

✓ Who will be responsible for inputting deals – the traders who commit to the deals or will you utilize trader deal tickets and have administrative assistants inputting deals?

✓ How will schedulers interact with each other in the system as the commodity moves from one area of responsibility to another, such as gas which might move from a Gulf Coast trading desk to a Midwest desk? How will that movement be managed, as some type of intra-company transfer or will you treat it as a "deal"? The implications will be important if your trading desks have separate P&L's.

✓ Who will coordinate/manage prior period adjustments and will that person or persons be responsible for the actual input of the adjustments?

Again, coming out of the implementation team training sessions, the team should have a preliminary idea as to the requirements that the new system implies. These ideas should be discussed amongst the team and a preliminary process map should be drafted. During the scenario testing phase, this map and assumptions should be tested, issues noted as arise, and alternatives explored. Upon completion of scenario testing, the new "rules" of system use should be fairly well established. Included in these new "rules" should be a security administration plan.

The security access area of the new system will need to be configured for each individual user ID. Access to view screens or the ability to input, update, or delete data elements must be established within the system, ultimately limiting individuals' access to only those areas that are necessary to complete their specific responsibilities. During the implementation process, but prior to parallel testing, it is not necessary to enact the security rules; however, it is important that they be established and ready to be enabled prior to parallel testing.

All of these "rules" and processes to be deployed in parallel testing and "live" production use should be fully documented and vetted as appropriate (reviewed and approved by the appropriate management and audit authorities).

While the activities of the Business Process Alignment are limited to addressing the process requirements of the system and ensuring the organization is aware of those requirements and positioned to address them, some companies may choose to also undertake a much broader Business Process Re-engineering (BPR) exercise in conjunction with the implementation process. The difference between the BPA and the BPR is scope: the BPA is focused only on making only those process changes mandated by the use of the new system. BPR's are generally considered to be much more wide-ranging activities that focus not only on the impacts of the new system, but also looks at the effectiveness and efficiencies of virtually every process associated with the organization, including management procedures, organizational structuring, corporate process interfaces, internal communication and even compensation practices. These engagements, due to their wide ranging scope and potential for massive process change are better left to be completed either well prior to or after the completion of the ETRM implementation.

o   **Parallel Testing** – Upon completion of testing, user training, and approval of all the processes associated with the new system, the customer should begin a process of parallel usage of the new system alongside their existing system(s). This period is critical to the successful use of the system, as this will be the time that the approved processes are "hardened" and the users become comfortable, not only with their abilities to use the system, but also in the ability of the system to manage their business. This period of parallel usage will require duplicative management of the customers business, meaning that every transaction will need to be captured twice, and every position or report reconciled new to old. Obviously this will be a trying time for all the users and will place strain on the organization. However, it is critical that parallel testing be performed, as the cost of cutting over from one system to the other without sufficient testing and proving could be catastrophic. While its generally recommended that the parallel period last for two successive and successful accounting periods, given the cost in terms of effort and organizational strain, many companies choose to limit parallel testing to successfully modeling a single accounting period.

o   **User Acceptance/Go Live** – The completion of parallel testing will generally mark "user acceptance", the milestone that indicates that the system has been successfully implemented. While this may seem to be in some ways an unnecessary formality, it is in fact an important milestone that indicates the users have signaled their willingness to "own" the system. It may also be a contractual milestone on which license or services payments are contingent.

A Brief Discussion of Fixed Price Implementations

Often companies buying a new ETRM will insist that the vendor or a third party consulting organization provide a fixed cost implementation, meaning that those vendors will supply a certain number of consulting resources for the term of the project and, regardless of the amount of time ultimately required to complete the project (as long as scope remains constant), they will not pay more than the originally negotiated price. This agreement has obvious appeal for the buyer in that they can limit their cost exposure. Additionally, many buyers feel that such an agreement will motivate the vendor or consultant to expedite the implementation project, after all, if they get done early, the come out ahead. Unfortunately, experience points to several issues with fixed price agreements.

In order to accurately price the implementation, the vendor must develop a highly granular project plan, one that details every task and activity. Using this plan, they will be able to estimate the amount of time required by their resources (plus some amount of contingency time) and apply a dollar rate to those hours in order to arrive at a price for which they believe they can deliver the project. The project plan will form the basis of all deliverables during the project and does not allow, without any extensive change control, any deviations from that plan. Unfortunately, given the complexity of ETRM products and the nature of the energy trading business, implementations will never proceed as originally envisioned and planned. Customer resource issues will arise where, due to a pressing business development or simply due to illness, a key resource in a critical path activity will not be available. Business processes described during the planning process will not be accurately mapped due to miscommunication between the vendor and the customer leading to significant analysis and remapping. Seemingly simple requests to change a field, or include a new one, on a custom report may require significant rewrites of code. In each of these cases, a fixed price project will require the vendor and the customer to agree to a change control and ultimately a price for the revised activities. While it seems a simple process, experience shows that these negotiations can be quite contentious and time consuming. Ultimately, fixed price implementations require significantly more project administration effort and have a much greater potential to spiral into overtly adversarial relationship between the parties. Given the commercial dependence and exposure each party has with, and to, the other, it would seem wise to limit the risks involved in the implementation and develop an agreement that facilitates a partnership, not an adversarial relationship.

CHAPTER 9

IMPLEMENTATION KEY SUCCESS FACTORS

Mr. Randall Orbon

Vice President, Trading and Risk Management,

Sapient

The increase in global energy demand has attracted a large number of new entrants into the energy trading industry who are hoping to reap profits from increased market volatility. Meanwhile, established incumbents are seeking to drive greater returns by optimizing their current portfolios through more sophisticated trading practices or expansion into new commodities, markets, and geographies. Physical and financial trading organizations continue to cross over into each other's realms, refining business processes and systems to support new trading strategies.

Overall market volatility, large volumes of capital from traditional energy trading organizations, and the emergence of hedge funds as energy trading players have driven increased interest in commodity and derivative trading and trading activity, making energy trading an increasingly challenging – and promising -- industry. Old methods no longer ensure success, and traders must employ innovative trading strategies supported by state-of-the-art tools to optimize portfolios and identify and exploit complex global market opportunities. Those that don't keep pace will likely operate at a disadvantage to their peers and may not be able to capitalize on as wide a range of trading opportunities.

Despite the trend towards greater operational efficiency, higher margins, and an ever increasingly competitive trading environment, many firms have yet to invest in adequate energy trading and risk management technologies. These firms continue to manage millions, if not billions, of dollars of market and credit risk on spreadsheets or outdated applications. However, some leaders in the industry are realizing that advanced information systems are critical to ensuring continued success in the new trading environment.

ETRM systems take the form of fully integrated, package-based or custom solutions; best-of-breed software packages with multiple system interfaces; or a series of manual processes supported by spreadsheets and paper forms. Smaller, newer firms may select manual processes and spreadsheets or ASP offerings for their cost and ease-of-implementation. Larger, more established trading operations typically opt for package or custom solutions to manage and integrate complex data sets and model risk effectively. Still others may consider reengineering legacy applications, a surprisingly costly and time-consuming process. Regardless of their approach, all companies will seek to maximize IT investments and ensure continued access to business processes and data. Additionally, all trading companies will want to ensure that their ETRM systems will grow with them, whether that means scaling with increased transaction loads or accommodating strategy shifts.

Energy Trading Value Chain

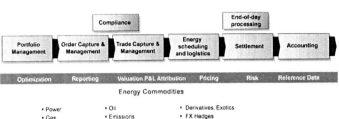

Energy Commodities

- Power
- Gas
- Coal

- Oil
- Emissions
- Refined Products

- Derivatives, Exotics
- FX Hedges
- Credit derivatives
- Weather derivatives

As companies seek partners for ETRM implementations, they should evaluate their industry and commodity expertise, skill developing solutions along the energy value chain, and experience with market-leading solution sets.

Despite vendor promises to the contrary, there is no single solution that will meet all of a trading company's needs without significant customization or manual work-arounds. Companies have unique trading strategies and proprietary analytics, and they vary considerably in terms of transactional complexity, trading volumes, organizational structure, and business requirements. Consequently, it is imperative that firms take the time to map their desired capabilities against vendor offerings, understanding the strengths and shortcomings of the different products. While an ETRM system is a significant investment, it is one that will only deliver optimal value with proper planning.

In this chapter, we profile several representative companies, the approaches they used to deliver on their business visions, and the systems that they selected to accomplish critical business objectives. In some cases, these profiles are based on a single client engagement, while other profiles represent multiple clients dealing with a similar situation. We have used pseudonyms throughout to protect the identities of all companies discussed in this chapter.

To aid firms in their planning, selection, and implementation of a world-class ETRM system, the following critical success factors are offered. These success factors were identified during interviews with project team members who have had repeated success in implementing

ETRM solutions worldwide to achieve a diverse range of client business goals.

Creating a Business Vision

What is your vision for your energy trading business? Are you seeking to optimize performance in existing markets or expand into new ones? What is unique about your approach to market: Are you driving for greater liquidity, seeking to add new assets, or trading new commodities? How complex is your business model and your market transactions? Is your model focused on risk management, asset optimization, or product arbitrage? Being clear with your partners about your desired trading goals and the successes and limitations of your current approach will help you craft an effective strategy and design a system to optimize your trading portfolio and mitigate risk. Conversely, being unclear could result in additional costs or substandard performance, as vendors will need to retrofit the system to address your needs. Your business vision should also articulate what success will look like as you implement an ETRM system. Start narrowing scope by answering these questions: What are your user requirements? What are the budget and timeline? What business measures should be achieved? And what rate of adoption are you seeking to achieve?

It's important to move beyond quick fixes to current pain points and craft a business vision that considers future growth, whether it is an increase in trading volume; the need to respond to regulatory changes; or a move into new geographies, commodities, or instruments. ETRM implementations represent sizeable investments, can take months or even years to fully implement, and are typically used for at least five to seven years to defray their cost of ownership. A company that considers only current requirements will run the risk of installing a system that will quickly become obsolete, frustrating business users and short-circuiting return on investment.

Our examples demonstrate a wide range of business visions:

Amerex, a global oil broker and trader, desired to integrate its financial and physical trading activities into one system to improve risk management capabilities and reporting. Furthermore, the company's existing system failed to support business growth and was based on an older technology that was difficult to manage and upgrade. The company sought to improve its handling of different deal types and its hedging capabilities, while leveraging new risk measures and analytics for superior performance. Additionally, Amerex wanted to automate routine processes which required extensive manual intervention, thus adding cost, complexity, and error to financial reporting.

Investa, an investment bank, sought to replace legacy applications inherited with the acquisition of a marketer's natural gas trading book. The legacy applications couldn't scale with the business and were based on an environment that was losing support in the latest Windows Operating System release, so Investa needed to move swiftly. To make the most of its investment, Investa decided to integrate its power, crude, agriculture, metals, and emissions commodities into a single platform and evolve its natural gas trading logistics, so that it could focus scheduling staff on higher-level activities.

Energy Forward, an energy merchant, sought to understand its multi-commodity portfolio and corresponding risks in a far more comprehensive manner than was possible with its existing system. With the acquisition of a gas market supplier, Energy Forward had inherited several offices and multiple ETRM systems, increasing data management complexity and fragmenting its view of risk. The company needed to combine its natural gas production sales and power generation facilities trading into a single, uniform software platform to create superior physical and financial trading and risk management capabilities.

EuroEnergyStar Group, a European energy company sought to prepare for coming deregulation by improving business processes and data handling. The company managed massive data volumes to meet its country's regulatory reporting requirements. Believing that it could leverage new data insights into better decision making and increased revenue, the company committed to a major trading transformation initiative. The multi-year initiative encompassed redesigned business processes, a unified system architecture for all utility services, a new data warehouse, and the integration of more than 20 business applications. Realizing that gains from this initiative would take longer to achieve, EuroEnergyStar also deployed select applications, such as a gas optimization application, to achieve quick wins while positioning the company to capitalize on emerging business opportunities.

New Vista Trading, a hedge fund that sought to expand its energy derivatives trading volume exponentially, needed to implement a front-to-back ETRM solution quickly. In addition, the company wanted to expand the solution over time to deliver complex data analytics to trader desktops in an easy-to-use format that allowed traders to capitalize on market opportunities on a real-time basis. While New Vista Trading needed the system to be up and running quickly, it planned to migrate to a more customized solution over time.

Finding a Trusted Advisor

Many trading companies choose to partner with a consulting firm to help them craft an effective strategy; understand their options across business processes, technical infrastructure, and data management; and develop an implementation approach that will meet their business objectives. It's critical to find a partner who is committed to your success. That partner will help you explore the full range of factors involved in your system implementation and provide candid insights about the successes and shortcomings of various approaches. It's not just about replacing a system; it's about driving your company to the next level. This relationship is first tested in the contracting process. Is the partner willing to commit to a fixed price for the next phase of work? And is the company willing to accept fees based on the accomplishment of specific business goals and tangible measurable milestones? If not, that should be a red flag and an impetus to keep searching for a partner whose motivations mirror your own.

Your partner will help push the project forward and make sure everyone on the team – company business executives and technologists, vendors, and external consultants – are all aligned around the business vision. This company should be a consulting firm that has a demonstrated track record in solving companies' business challenges and developing ETRM systems that drive results. This expertise should be highly relevant to the business and technology challenges you currently face. For example, a consulting firm that is hired to develop a specific commodity trading solution should have deep experience in that specific commodity and all relevant technologies used to optimize the trading process. Of equal importance, your partner should have a history of building long-term relationships with both clients and vendors, indicating that they are successful at delivering industry-leading results and at bringing the right vendors to the table.

A partner's industry expertise should be backed by a diverse service mix, so that you have access to the full suite of services you need, such as business and IT strategy, business intelligence, and outsourced support and maintenance. Pragmatic innovators will also offer reusable tools and components, allowing you to benefit from previous client successes and creatively solve pressing problems that aren't addressed effectively by current market offerings.

Obviously trust is earned, not given. Companies often select a consulting partner on the basis of their expertise. However, consultants should bring more than a solid track record to a new project. They should also bring excellent communication skills; an ability to develop a personal rapport with client staff; and values, such as honesty, client-focused delivery, and a genuine investment in their partner's success to the engagement – all qualities that help build trust over time. A common pitfall is to dilute accountability across an array of consultants and internal staff. Find the right partner and make sure they are willing to take full accountability for the team's delivery.

Assembling the Right Talent

How do you know if you have the right project team? Evaluate the talent pool. Each member of the team should bring expertise solving relevant client business challenges and implementing similar systems. Many firms will present an industry expert, but staff a team with junior industry professionals. Make sure your partner's team has experience. Having implemented similar systems, this team will know how to structure initiatives, avoid common pitfalls, evaluate vendors, and communicate and manage change effectively. A common pitfall is to wait until too late in the process to apply the right experience.

Designing book structures, asset valuation mechanisms, and trade execution strategies are all examples of things that should be handled by experts and set up correctly from the beginning. The right team will help you assess the business process changes you've thought of, as well as the ones you haven't.

Where are your team members located? Is your partner willing to bring the right talent to the right location for this initiative? When EuroEnergyStar embarked on its multi-year, transformation initiative, its partner brought in energy experts from the United States and United Kingdom – countries that had experienced deregulation several years previously. As a consequence, team members were savvy about what lay ahead for their client. For the Investa project, the partner brought logistics experts to the client site.

A good partner knows when to go outside the consulting firm to seek out specific expertise. An example of this is organizational change management. Rather than rebranding a business analyst or project manager as a change management expert, a consulting firm may do well to find an external expert who has helped many other organizations assess their readiness for change, craft a detailed change management plan, and implement the full set of customized tools needed to achieve desired objectives.

Another hallmark of a good partner is one who can help companies identify new business opportunities they haven't considered, streamline operations, or pinpoint areas of outside risk the company may not have considered. While Investa knew it needed to improve its transport function, the company didn't realize that automating this function would help create a new revenue stream. The company's new logistics system uses rules-based engines and historical data to make critical, accurate pre-scheduling assumptions, freeing up schedulers to accomplish higher-level tasks such as identifying and selling excess transport capacity. Meanwhile, Amerex knew how vital it was to have experienced personnel on their trading package selection and implementation project. The company selected a partner based on the consultant's track record of delivering these systems on-time and on-budget, a qualification other vendors were not able to demonstrate for a project of that size or complexity. After the package was implemented, Amerex realized that the current method for delegating authority to the traders was not an accurate reflection of the market risk the company faced. The partner helped devise a plan for converting the new system to measure delegation of authority in a more accurate manner and provide the information upper management needed to evaluate this change.

Exploring Your Options

Most companies evaluate the following set of options when seeking to modernize their trading systems: upgrade an existing legacy system, implement a new end-to-end package solution, build a custom solution, or design a hybridized system that leverages some or all of these approaches. The costs and benefits of these different options vary significantly. While improving legacy systems seems to make sense in some cases, it often proves cost-prohibitive or infeasible due to the limitations of the underlying technology or inadequate architecture. Package solutions require less time to implement and offer an attractive price point compared to custom systems; however, companies often sacrifice functionality that meets their unique needs due to the cost, unwillingness, or inability of vendors to customize package solutions to perform clients' desired business processes.

Regardless of which approach they implement, companies need to analyze how proposed packages integrate with existing platforms and the level of complexity they create to determine which solutions will provide maximum return on investment. Package solutions are often implemented by trading organizations whose business is straightforward and does not require costly customization or by companies who do not have the need or capital to customize packages. What's critical is to "get smart" about your needs and package capabilities as quickly as possible, so that you can devote ample time to analyzing the pros and cons of customizing a package versus creating a custom application for your trading needs.

In these examples, the companies had existing systems in place when they started the ETRM evaluation process. Consequently, they understood the gaps between what their existing systems provided and what their current requirements necessitated. Most were seeking to improve clearly defined processes, which helped the companies carefully evaluate available options. Many needed help in defining their future state needs and thus found great value from teaming with a partner with a vision for the future of energy trading and deep insights gained from a vast number of past system deployments.

During this phase, a trading company will conduct a thorough vendor evaluation. If the company has specialized needs or wants to look at only market leaders, this may be a relatively focused process. Some companies, however, may want to be methodical about how they evaluate options. Amerex evaluated integrated end-to-end solutions, best-of-breed solutions, and the pros and cons of updating its legacy solution, assessing more 80 solutions and solution components that could potentially meet its complex transactional needs.

How can companies make this process as effective and painless as possible?

- Work with your partner to use business objectives to drive a rapid analysis of all relevant business processes, identify gaps between the current state and business vision, and design an architecture vision and roadmap

- Use knockout criteria to narrow the list of choices as quickly as possible. For example, a company trading natural gas will seek a vendor with that specific expertise; a company that offers a generic trading system may not offer the features needed to support physical natural gas trading.

- Prioritize requirements, so that you understand what criteria are non-negotiable and what are optional.

- Assess the vendor's capabilities against your future state vision, to make sure that the solution will grow with your trading operations.

- Leverage your partner's knowledge of the space to assess candidates and develop probing questions about capabilities.

- Research the vendor's experience, finances, and strategy, to make sure the company has the right qualifications and decision making – from R&D investments to key partnerships – that will keep the product at the forefront of the industry in terms of innovation and market responsiveness.

- Set up conference room pilots, where business users run scenarios, interact with functionality, and assess system integration, while IT personnel evaluate the integrity and scalability of the organization. Use this information to score solutions both quantitatively and qualitatively.

- Involve the technology and business team in all aspects of the solution selection, so that staff can make an educated decision and make sure that the system meets their full set of requirements.

- Track vendor interactions. Are personnel responsive and easy to work with? How do they respond to change? How do they escalate issues? And how do their personnel fit with your corporate culture? If you choose this vendor, you will interact with the company's staff for five to seven years—or even longer. It's important that there be a good fit.

- Check vendor references. Probe on how they resolved issues and frequency of releases. Evaluate other clients' interaction with the firm, not just their satisfaction with the product.

What choices did our trading companies make?

Energy Forward wanted to understand its portfolio and corresponding risks in a more comprehensive, flexible, and visual manner than was possible with best-of-breed products. Consequently, it decided to commit to a largely custom solution built around an off-the-shelf trade capture system that would provide it with superior market and credit risk management. The company worked with its partner to build an enterprise-wide, multi-commodity data warehouse and risk reporting and analytics solution. The data warehouse would provide a consolidated and flexible view of all of the company's positions, curves, volatilities, counterparties, locations, and strategies, and maintain a year's worth of archival data available for simulations and reporting. Additionally, the company built a customized risk modeling engine that calculated the firm's profit and loss (P&L), value-at-risk (VaR), and potential forward exposure (PFE) on a daily basis. Previously, the company had used gross margin at risk to optimize its physical portfolio, but had no way of doing that with its marketing and trading portfolio. With the data that was now available from the new solution, Energy Forward was able to build a robust optimization engine that integrated existing positions, various risk scenarios, and the characteristics of each of the company's power plants to optimize its trading portfolio based on the physical assets that the company controlled.

New Vista Trading knew that the most critical part of the new solution was going to be the interface that traders had with the system, since the company planned to extend and replace various parts of the middle and back office functionality over time. Consequently, New Vista Trading worked with its partner to understand the pros and cons of the various packages available. Once the company had reduced the list to a set of packages that could provide it with enough architectural flexibility to extend the solution as needed over time, New Vista Trading began to work directly with its traders to assess the usability of each of the short-listed applications. The traders quickly focused in on one specific application that they felt was the optimal fit with their front office needs. New Vista Trading assembled a small team of experts to evaluate the selected product and implemented a completely out-of-the-box implementation relatively quickly. Once this solution was up and running, the company worked with its partner to define and implement a set of enhancements, customizations, and ancillary tools to optimize the solution to meet ongoing trading strategy needs.

To meet regulatory demands, EuroEnergyStar rapidly selected and implemented an ETRM system for power as a short-term solution. As EuroEnergyStar explored its options for building unified system architecture, it measured every decision against four strategic objectives – whether it would comply with its clearly defined technology future state, provide freedom from vendor lock-in, support product lifecycles of a year or less, and help the company maintain good business processes. EuroEnergyStar evaluated 30 different vendors and a custom solution. After narrowing the field to two finalists, the company realized that any single package would require significant customization. EuroEnergyStar selected one package to act as its core platform and worked with its partner to create the infrastructure architecture, technical architecture, and common data model that would provide straight-through processing and maximize standardization. Working top down, the two companies created principles to identify when applications should be custom-built and when packages could be deployed. Those principles are still used for application development today.

While moving forward with its large-scale transformation, EuroEnergyStar also implemented point solutions to solve pressing challenges. One such challenge involved gas trading, where reporting tools lagged behind trading volume, and traders had little support to decide whether their trades were profitable. EuroEnergyStar custom-built a gas optimization system that integrated deal capture, demand forecasting, gas nominations, contracts, a storage calculator, transport capacity, and weather forecast, providing real-time visibility across the entire gas portfolio. Traders were able to improve their effectiveness, and the company generated a position and optimized position report daily.

Managing for Change

Acquire executive buy-in early on in the project, to ensure ongoing commitment to the initiative, sufficient budget, and the ability to make decisions when issues escalate. Allocate the right personnel for the initiative and set up the appropriate project oversight, defining reporting and governance mechanisms, communications protocols, and work processes. Clearly define roles and make sure that the team is vertically integrated, to ensure that all project team members from all aspects of the business and all firms represented are working together to effectively move the project forward. Where possible, align drivers so that team members are incented to work together. Involve business users early, so that they have ownership of the solution and a stake in

119

its success. Your users should help define requirements, evaluate vendors, participate in key decisions, test the system, and serve as its champions when you are rolling it out. In short, they should serve as true collaborators in defining, designing, and deploying your ETRM system.

Optimizing Delivery

Since a significant portion of the costs associated with an ETRM system is the labor required to integrate it into your current technology environment, look for options that lower cost without sacrificing quality. One option is to engage a partner who offers offshore development expertise. Carefully evaluate working processes. How will the team be structured to ensure that the project is optimally allocated among key team members? What functions will reside in the local geography, and what functions will be performed offshore? How will the team communicate internally and with you, the client? How will they escalate issues for effective resolution? How will they share information and best practices to leverage insights gained on past assignments?

Effective teams will have worked out communication and collaboration issues ahead of the time, so that the project will proceed seamlessly. Additionally, many will offer "quick-start" capabilities, so that the project can move rapidly through the requirements gathering phase.

Additionally, you may want to explore different delivery approaches such as Agile development, which can improve speed-to-market, while reducing risk and cost. By breaking system implementations into small chunks of functionality, Agile, or iterative, development reduces cycle times while providing companies with production-grade software they can implement quickly. In addition, it increases quality and flexibility, enabling trading companies to adapt readily to changing requirements. What's critical is to pair Agile with the right amount of project management to keep project teams focused and accountable.

Agile development can be performed on a fixed-time, fixed-price model, allowing companies to benefit from rapid development while staying within cost and time objectives. The consulting company works with the client on each iteration to define and price new requirements, providing the client with ongoing visibility and the flexibility to make changes and tradeoffs to accomplish critical goals.

Several of the companies we profiled used Agile development to roll out new functionality early in the development process, either to use a test-and-learn approach to refine business requirements or provide traders with tools they could use to exploit market growth. One company, Investa, used Agile development to gain business buy-in and show users how their feedback was incorporated. This was done first by quickly selecting a package based directly on traders' input and implementing it aggressively without customization. The ETRM system was then rolled out to production so that traders could immediately use new functionality and increase their effectiveness. Once the system was up and running, bundles of enhancements and customizations were rolled out to production on a regular basis. The business quickly realized that this was a completely different approach from traditional "big bang" waterfall development engagements and that if something wasn't right in the application, it could be quickly addressed in upcoming releases. Through this process, business users saw that their needs and priorities had a direct impact on what was delivered to their desktops.

Achieving the Right Results

So what were some of the results? We share results from several of the companies we profiled:

Amerex measured its ETRM system results in terms of both its improved unit cost and its operational efficiency. The company realized a 3% decrease in G&A cost per mmbtu and significantly reduced manual intervention and error, cutting the time required to gather risk data for reporting price and trade violations by 88% and reducing manual errors in financial systems by 75%. In addition, the company was able to redeploy 60% of back office staff on front or mid-office functions and release 30 contractors when their contracts expired.

Energy Forward consolidated three ETRM systems into a single platform, creating a single point of entry for the trade capture of physical and financial power and gas transactions. The company then built a corporate position, profit and loss, and credit application using one data model, increasing trading accuracy and visibility. Energy Forward used this information to capitalize on new opportunities, stabilize the environment, and ultimately sell its natural gas division.

Investa folded eight legacy systems and four vendor applications into a single ETRM platform, creating straight-through processes and reducing its technology cost of ownership. The company added commodities to its trading desk, creating the flexibility it needed to scale the business and automating thousands of transactions each day. Investa plans to implement a single uniform trade capture system for all commodities as a precursor to rolling its commodities trading business into its equities trading environment, which will allow the company to offer expanded services to retail clients.

EuroEnergyStar, which invested substantial investment of time, personnel, and resources in one of the industry's largest-scale transformation initiatives, was confident the initiative would pay for itself within two years, an accomplishment it easily achieved. The company achieved realized an even more dramatic result with its gas optimization application. The system paid for itself within several daily nominations of installation by improving traders' ability to capitalize on market volatility and eliminating regulatory penalties for gas transportation mismanagement.

Maximizing System Adoption

As mentioned above, companies that are successful in driving adoption involve key stakeholders throughout the ETRM system implementation process. If business users help define requirements, provide hands-on feedback on solution finalists, offer input on the implementation process, and participate in training that is customized for their needs, they will likely be strong advocates of the system selected. While IT staff will be integrally involved throughout the implementation process, adoption can be a challenge for this group as well, if staff are confronted with unfamiliar approaches, such as a different delivery methodology. Involving both groups throughout the project is critical to gaining credibility and acceptance of new processes and systems.

122

Additionally, communication is critical. Start early and maintain focus on the business vision, while providing stakeholders with ongoing updates on progress, roadblocks, and the path forward will build people's comfort level in decision making. Equally importantly, the team must develop an effective escalation strategy and then deliver on it to make sure that issues are raised with the right decision makers and resolved quickly.

As an example, Energy Forward began making comprehensive, up-to-date risk information available to its business users each day and making key decisions using system data. The company's two-fold approach – of providing value to individual traders and reinforcing the system's importance on a corporate level – made system adoption extremely successful.

Amerex utilized a formal organizational change management approach to ensure adoption. Plans for communication, learning, change readiness, and stakeholder engagement were created at the beginning of the project and executed by dedicated staff to ensure that the organization was prepared for the change ahead. Application preview sessions allowed users to see progress in the development of the user interface, the part of the system they cared about most, keeping business commitment to the multi-year transformation initiative high. The supervisory team met on a regular basis to discuss major cross-functional issues. Project business analysts, who were taken from the trading organization, helped develop training materials specifically targeted to their groups' activities. The training was so effective that it was subsequently used to onboard new staff in both the IT and business organizations. Embedding an operational change management function within the initiative ensured that this important issue was considered from day one, enabling the project team and executive team to head off potential issues and ensuring a successful rollout of the application to the business and IT organizations.

Conclusion

Implementing an effective ETRM system is a significant priority for many industry players, yet the path forward is far from clear. Trading companies must evaluate their business requirements and traders' needs against an often bewildering set of options. Additionally, they must chart a course that effectively circumnavigates potential pitfalls, while keeping the implementation on-track. Fortunately, trading companies have a valuable ally in the form of consulting partners. The right partners will bring highly relevant expertise to ETRM engagements, helping companies rapidly cut through industry noise to plan, design, and implement a system that is the best fit for their current trading needs and future growth plans. Additionally, the right partners will demonstrate that they are invested in their clients' success with everything they do, creating the foundation for a long-lasting relationship that delivers results. As trading firms move forward with costly, time-consuming ETRM projects, it is reassuring to many that they can leverage the expertise of true partners to accomplish their business goals. While we have presented many success factors in this chapter, we believe that selecting the right partner is the most critical one of them all and can help companies reap maximum value from their ETRM system implementations.

CHAPTER 10

THE IMPLEMENTATION TEAM

Mr. Patrick Reames,

UtiliPoint International, Inc.

"Choose the right people for the job" is a truism, and just good common sense. Selecting the right individuals, with the right mix of knowledge, skills, and "get it done" attitude is an absolute necessity for an ETRM implementation project. Given the cost of a potential failure and the importance of the application to the business, it would seem patently insane not to dedicate the best resources, those that are most likely to ensure success, to the project. Unfortunately, it doesn't always happen.

At UtiliPoint, we conduct numerous studies and surveys, many looking at ETRM product implementations. In our research and general involvement in the industry, we come across many examples of failed implementations. In the recent cases of project failure, we've seen a common thread – the projects were not executed properly. That's not to say that there were not contributing factors, such as code issues that proved difficult to resolve, as these types of issues will always complicate a project. Generally, and our own experiences bear this out, projects fail because the right people weren't involved or, those that were involved lacked the capabilities or, will to make the project a success.

Project Ownership - Business, Not IT

For a company undertaking an ETRM implementation project, it's tempting to look to the IT organization to lead. After all, that's what they do – they install software. In fact, in many organizations, the IT department is home to project managers, network and database administrators, and software developers. On the surface, IT is a perfect fit for the job - and for many software projects, IT is the best bet for success – however, ETRM systems are unique in that the entirety of the commercial operations of an energy trading enterprise is dependent upon that system. ETRM systems capture and manage all the commercial agreements including trades; they manage and optimize logistics; they provide analytics and business intelligence from which decisions are made to commit hundreds of millions of dollars; they manage counter-party credit exposures; at the end of the day, they take care of all the associated accounting for every transaction. ETRM systems are truly **mission-critical** applications, and it is the business users that are staking their careers on the successful use of the application.

A company's ETRM system must be a reflection of the business group using it. Given the complexity of the business processes and the intensity of data involved, ETRM systems are **implemented**, not just installed, solutions. These systems must be configured through an extensive process of data loading, business process mapping, scenario testing and user training (*see Implementations – Chapter 8)*. As such, the implementation process requires the active involvement, support, and, yes, *ownership* by those business users that will rely on the system everyday to make decisions, that if wrong, could create significant financial losses for their company.

Sources of Resources

Most implementation teams are a combination of skills and experience from one or more of the following sources – customer resources, vendor resources, and third party consulting companies. No implementation should be undertaken without a minimum of client supplied business knowledge and vendor supplied product knowledge, and depending on the project goals and scope, it may be appropriate to bring in expertise not readily available except from third party consulting organizations. These skills would include business process re-engineering, large scale application development, and business strategy consulting.

Vendor Supplied Resources

Every product vendor has a staff of knowledgeable professional consultants with skills in business process modeling, training, installation and technical skills such as development, report writing and integration. These vendor supplied resources should supplement your implementation team, not supplant it. Do not expect your selected vendor to implement the product for you – even if they could know all the intricacies of your business and perfectly model those in your new acquired system, once they completed that configuration, your business would be left in the dark as to how to use the system and how to manage future business in it.

One of the greatest advantages of employing vendor resources on your project is that in addition to deep product knowledge, they can bring with them the experiences of other clients - how those others have addressed issues that you will face, such as how do you capture transportation optionality, how do you synchronize contact databases that may exist in multiple different systems, how do you manage development of custom reports? These are issues that many users have faced in the past, issues for which there may be no simple answer. It's the combined experiences of dozens of clients of your selected vendor, channeled through that vendor's consulting staff, which will help you answer these questions

Your vendor will also be the best source for product specific technical knowledge – data models, integration points, data mart strategies, etc. They will have an intimate knowledge of the code and a broad base of experience in various methods and technologies that may be deployed for integration and reporting.

Always seek to maintain consistent resources during the term of the implementation process. Work with your selected vendor to identify the right resources upfront and keep them actively involved in your project. If your project is subject to starts and stops as your internal team switches focus back and forth from part-time involvement in the implementation project to their full-time business responsibilities, you will be inclined to send the vendor resources back to their office in order to minimize your costs. If you do this, you're going to have a hard time keeping those same people involved in your project. Those resources are a significant part of the vendor's revenue stream. If you're not using them, the vendor will, understandably, move those consultants on to other projects. If that happens, you're going to be faced with having to educate the new consultants on the ins and outs of your business, further delaying your project and costing you additional money in the process - just another good reason to keep your project moving ahead by assigning your internal resources to your project on a full-time, dedicated basis.

Third Party Resources

Third party consultants, sometimes known as system integrators, can be of significant value, particularly in the more complex and wide ranging projects. These consulting organizations will generally have broad expertise in not only the relevant technologies, but they also will be able to bring expertise in the product being implemented.

In our research and experience, these third party groups have been successful in providing valuable assistance in areas such as business process mapping and re-engineering, systems integration, project management assistance, and, occasionally, supplemental staffing to free up client resources to more actively participate in the implementation project. For a more in-depth discussion of the use of third party consultants, or systems integrators, see Chapter 11.

Hybrid Organizations

In some of the larger energy trading organizations, "hybrid" ETRM support groups have emerged. These groups form a dedicated IT support team for the energy trading organizations and their mission critical software applications. Their leaders are many times Director level positions with titles along the lines of "Director of Trading Systems". These groups are generally staffed with individuals that have at some point served in the business unit, but have shown a affinity for technology and have transitioned to the support group, bringing with them significant business knowledge.

These trading support groups will normally be dependent upon the IT organization for their budgets and will therefore answer up to the CIO of the company. However, in most, there is also a "dotted line" reporting relationship to the head of the energy trading commercial unit.

Experience has shown these types of organizations have been very successful in not only supplying key members to the implementation team, but also in providing primary support for the users of the ETRM system after it goes live. For organizations that can afford to deploy this type of an internal support group, the benefits are significant. However, these teams of resources cannot be expected to do the work in isolation. Even with these hybrid organizations, active involvement of the business users is required. Energy trading is a dynamic business and without the involvement of the front-line resources supplying their most current knowledge and expressing their requirements, the project will never meet their expectations.

Client Resources – Full-time vs. Part-time

Perhaps the most common mistake made by companies implementing an ETRM system is not providing full-time dedication of resources to the project. In many cases, the company will provide for a full-time project manager, but the other resources will be allocated on a part-time basis. While this type of arrangement has been marginally successful for very small businesses, those with less than a dozen or so employees; when larger businesses attempt to "part-time" their projects, it usually results in some degree of failure, either total failure where the project is never completed, or partial failures – those where the project was well over budget in terms of time and dollars, or was not fully implemented, leaving the business users with a crippled or incomplete system.

It is unfortunately very common for a company to tell the assigned resources that they are going to continue in their current roles, but they need to make time to work on the implementation. When they ask how that's supposed to work, being that they are 100% employed in doing what they do, they're told something along the lines of "we'll see what we can do to get you some help". It's no wonder that in these types of situations, the people assigned to implementation projects rarely welcome the opportunity. They have picked up a huge additional work burden; they have to continue to do their current jobs; and they know that no matter how they try to balance the two, they will never be able to do both well. Clearly, as the implementation project is of limited duration, and as they are being judged on how well they do the jobs they were initially hired for, the implementation project is going to always get secondary attention.

In any complex project, momentum and consistent progress are keys in bringing the project to a successful conclusion. Supplying resources on a part-time or "best efforts" basis will most likely stall progress and can cause the project to flounder, driving costs up and delaying or endangering the project's success.

If your organization cannot afford to supply experienced, skilled resources on a full-time basis, you should probably re-examine your decision to pursue acquisition of a large scale ETRM system and delay the purchase until your organization is properly staffed and structured.

Client Resources - Characteristics for Success

When selecting team members to work on an implementation project, you need to identify those that have the right mix of characteristics necessary to implement a complex system. These characteristics are:

- Ability – Intelligent and can quickly solve complex problems.

- Experience – For business team members, a deep knowledge of their role and at least a solid working knowledge of one other functional role. For technology team members, solid experience with the relevant technologies that they will be working with. All team members should be relatively skilled in the use of MS Office.

- Attitude – willingness to work hard, be adaptable to change, and be a leader for change in their area of responsibility. Being open minded is vitally important – a willingness to see other ways of achieving the same result. Not being flexible and open minded, that is trying to stick with the 'we have always done it this way' mentality can cause delays and unnecessary work arounds.

In some cases, a company will assign junior resources to their implementation project, figuring that their most experienced are too valuable to pull out of the daily business. We would advocate the best path would be to apply your most experienced people to ensuring the new system is the best possible reflection of your current and future business. The project could then be an opportunity to challenge your junior staff, giving them the business experience necessary to grow into more responsible rolls

Strong Executive Support and Oversight

Having dedicated, highly skilled technical and business resources to do the "heavy lifting" of an implementation goes a long way to ensuring a successful conclusion. However, it's not enough.

UtiliPoint asked a number of the thought leaders in the ETRM solutions space the following question: "Acknowledging that there are a number of critical elements to ensuring a successful outcome for an ETRM project, what do you feel is the most important element?" Of the 13 responses, 10 of them noted, in their opinion, the single most important element for ensuring project success is a strong executive mandate, and active participation and support from the executive sponsor.

Clearly, based upon these responses, no organization should undertake the implementation of an ETRM system without ensuring the organization, top to bottom, is properly aligned to, and supportive of, project scope and goals. Active executive involvement is clearly a key. The organization's leadership must unambiguously support the project and actively encourage the participation of all stakeholders in the process. It falls upon them to ensure key personnel are properly incentivized to not only participate, but to own both the project and its result. Executive management must lead this process, not merely react to issues that may arise. They should be in front of the project, proactively eliminating internal barriers and quickly resolving conflicts.

Building the Team

An implementation team is a hierarchically structured group of people from various sources that possess the necessary skills and knowledge that in their entirety provides the leadership, business knowledge, technical knowledge and organizational skills to move your newly purchased product from being just a piece of software to being an integral and invaluable asset to your company.

The typical construction of the implementation project team is shown in Figure 1 below and described in the following paragraphs.

Figure 1

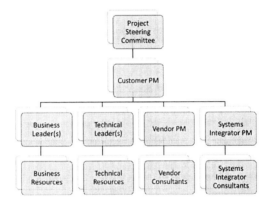

Project Steering Committee

If the ETRM product is being deployed in a company composed of multiple business units that may be impacted by the implementation (such as utilities or oil and gas producers), it would be appropriate to form a Project Steering Committee comprised of the executive leaders of those impacted groups.

The function and responsibilities of the Steering Committee will include:

- Ensure proper allocation and availability of staff resources
- Resolve policy issues

- Review and endorse business practice changes/adjustments
- Manage expectations within responsible business units
- Facilitate cross unit communication
- Review performance vs. budget

The project steering committee should be initiated prior to product selection and should continue to meet at least monthly during the life of the project. In many organizations, the steering committee will continue to function even after the new solution has gone into production.

<u>Follow the Right Leader – the Project Manager</u>

It's difficult to overstate the value that professional project management brings to an implementation. Having the right person with the necessary skills and experience in managing complex projects is a requirement to ensure the project remains on track when the inevitable issues arise. It's not enough to just have someone who can make assign tasks from a project plan. The real value of a good project manager is their ability to adjust, and in some cases improvise, when the plan goes off track due to issues outside of your control.

In most implementations, the project manager will be responsible for:

- Development and maintenance of the project plan
- Leadership of the project team, with the project leads answering directly to the PM
- Communicating status both vertically and horizontally across the organization
- Escalating issues that require executive attention/resolution
- Interfacing with the product vendor(s)
- Motivating team members and ensuring active participation by all

The project manager should be identified and assigned to the role as early in the process as possible and should be actively involved in the product selection phase.

UtiliPoint recommends that ETRM projects be headed by a Project Management Institute (PMI) certified project manager, commonly referred to a PMP or Project Management Professional certification. What does that mean? It means that individual has completed a full curriculum of training in project management skills and techniques, giving them the necessary tools to lead a large scale implementation project to success.

If your organization doesn't have an appropriately skilled individual on staff to lead the project, experienced project managers can be brought in on a contract basis. In selecting a contact project manager, always look for an appropriate certification, such as PMI/PMP, and a resume that indicates he or she has significant experience in projects similar to yours.

Keep in mind that **your** project manager should work for **your** company, not be an employee of the vendor or a third party consulting groups that may also be working as part of the implementation team. There will invariably be conflicts that arise and it is essential that your project manager is always mindful of, and looking out for, your best interests. Even the appearance of a potential conflict of interest could potentially exacerbate issues that arise. Your vendor of choice should provide a project manager that can provide guidance and assistance to your project manager, however the vendor's project manager should report to your project manager.

Team Leaders

If the scope and scale of the implementation project are large enough, implementation teams may employ team leaders aligned to the primary activity streams – technical, business, and development (if applicable). Under this structure, these team leaders would have the following responsibilities:

- Assist the Project Manager in developing, monitoring and updates the project plan.
- Operate as the primary project contact and escalation point for all resources within their respective activity streams
- Ensure the scheduling and availability of internal, vendor and third party resources as necessary to meet project goals.
- Escalate any issues that arise that may impact timelines and/or project success.
- Assume responsibility for motivating team member and maintaining project momentum

Functional Area Representation

Ensuring active participation by each functional area impacted by the new ETRM product is not only valuable to ensuring a successful implementation of the system, but is also vitally important in achieving buy-in to the new solution by the various business and technical units. Examples of the various groups that should be represented on the implementation team include:

- Contract Management
- Trading/Marketing
- Deal Origination
- Risk Management
- Scheduling
- Settlement
- Accounting
- Information Technology
  - o Reports Developers
  - o DBA/Network Administrators

Keep Your Team Motivated

During the project, motivation of the project team can become an issue. Rarely are implementations going to be considered "fun" by all of the team members. As large scale ETRM projects can easily extend for a year or more, it's important to keep the team motivated and moving toward a successful conclusion.

Participation on an implementation project team should never be detrimental to a team member, either financially or terms of their career progression. The best way to de-motivate someone is to tell them that their new job is to spend late hours working on a project that, while important to the company, will ultimately mean they don't qualify for their usual bonus or that the next promotion will be delayed because they aren't going to be doing their usual job for the duration of the project. It's vitally important that those who are participating on the project team view that participation as an opportunity to grow their skills and increase their value to the company, and at the same time not take a hit to their financial wellbeing.

Successful achievement of milestones should be celebrated within your company and team members rewarded accordingly. Make certain that the entire company knows what's going happening in terms of the progress and be sure everyone recognizes the hard work and sacrifice the team members are making to improve the ability of the company to remain competitive in the market. Experience has shown that the most successful implementation projects have been those where the team successes were noted and celebrated within the organization.

Conclusion

Regardless of your organization's size, if you have made the commitment to deploy a new ETRM system, you have, by extension, made the decision to risk large amounts of your company's resources— personnel, dollars, time, and opportunity. If successful, you will realize the benefit of having a system that will add real value to your business in terms of better decision making, improved efficiency, regulatory compliance, improved record keeping, etc. If unsuccessful, not only will you not realize these benefits, but you will have lost time, money, opportunity and quite possibly, the willingness of your organization to try again.

So, choose your team carefully. Weigh the costs of committing your best and brightest to the project versus the costs of a project that never ends, one that is a continual drain on company resources and employee morale.

Seek outside assistance when appropriate. The dollars spent upfront to bring in the right knowledge and experience are dollars with will be repaid in multiples after the conclusion of an efficient and effective project resulting in a fully and correctly implemented ETRM system.

CHAPTER 11

USING THIRD-PARTY INTEGRATORS

Dr. Gary M. Vasey,

UtiliPoint International, Inc.

Many ETRM projects utilize outside assistance in the form of third party consultants and Integration firms (that is resources supplied by companies other than the vendor or client). Using an integrator provides a level of additional expertise to the project team, supports and supplements the internal staff on the project, and can provide a tried and tested project management infrastructure to the project, amongst other benefits. Generally, the more complex the project, the more likely it is that an integrator will be used.

In a recent UtiliPoint survey on ETRM implementation, only about 30% of the ETRM implementation projects reflected in the survey did not use third party consultants for any purpose whatsoever. Of the other

70% of respondents, third party consultants and integrators were mostly used in the role of project manager/project office, followed by business process consulting, systems integration consulting, making enhancements and selection consulting.

The survey also showed that, although consultants were used on ETRM implementation projects of all durations and complexities, there is a correlation in the data between the use of consultants and total project duration. All projects lasting 12-months or more utilized outside consultants whereas only 50% of projects of less than 6-months duration used consultants. The survey data suggests that consultants are more likely to be used on longer and more complex ETRM implementation projects.

An interesting feature of the survey data (though this should be taken somewhat cautiously) is that the use of consultants on implementation projects did not appear to have a significant impact on either; overall project experience or, its perceived success. In fact, the data suggests that those who did not use a consulting or integration firm actually had a marginally better project experience than those that did. It would also appear that those that chose to implement themselves without external consulting assistance also had a greater success rate in terms of 'proper implementation'. It is important to note however, that it was generally smaller, less complex projects that were undertaken without external consulting assistance and the survey data undoubtedly reflects the decreased project complexity as opposed to providing any real conclusions about the use of outside consultants!

Figure 1: Project Experience With/Without Consultant Assistance

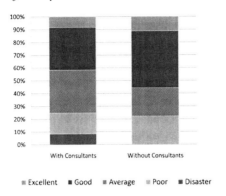

Whatever the practical experience of the use of integrators might be, it is a feature of the industry that integrators and consultants are often used in implementing and indeed, selecting ETRM software. In fact, some integration firms exclusively provide these services.

The Potential Benefits of Using an Integrator

There are innumerable potential benefits to using an integrator and some will depend upon the nature of the project and company undertaking the project. Nonetheless, some of the more obvious benefits fall into two areas:

Bringing in additional expertise

Most firms implementing an ETRM software solution are obviously actively engaged in trading energy commodities. While they may have an IT department, those staffs are often already overstretched and may not have sufficient expertise in the ETRM area. Similarly, the key end users are actively engaged in running the business day-to-day and it might not be feasible for them to be assigned fulltime to an implementation project. So an integrator can be used to bring in additional IT and business analyst resources to help undertake the project. UtiliPoint research demonstrates however that freeing up key end user staff to work on an ETRM implementation project is an essential ingredient in project success.

Perhaps as importantly however is that the integration firm will undoubtedly have worked on multiple ETRM implementation projects and will have a good deal of experience and expertise to share with its client. That expertise can help the company implementing a solution to avoid common errors in approach and reduce the overall risk of project failure. Furthermore, the integrator may even have familiarity and experience with the particular ETRM product being implemented again helping to reduce project risk but also supplementing the vendor's staff when it comes to understanding the ETRM solution.

Providing Method to Madness

Perhaps the most essential ingredient in a successful project is strong project management. Strong project management requires an experienced individual to act as project manager; one who can be forceful but act with tact while applying discipline to the process. Managing the various parties involved in the project is a key criteria to success and an ETRM implementation project can include a raft of business functions, external parties (the vendor(s) and so on) and egos and opinions. The project manager will bring together the diverse parties and ensure that they operate as a team.

In conjunction with project management is the project plan and overall methodologies and documentation used to manage the project. The integrator will bring a tried and tested methodology set to the table and be familiar with it. That set of methodologies will have processes, approaches and standard documentation to cover things such as change management, project planning and tracking and project management for example. The methodology will also focus on objectives, goals and milestones with a format and rules for determining when these have been met; all critical in IT projects as complex as implementing an ETRM software solution.

The integrator's toolkit will also contain experience and guidance on key project considerations such as data conversion approach, training approach, testing and the set up of the overall IT environment to successfully run the software. Additionally, they will bring to the table other critical items such as backup and recovery plans, upgrade planning, security and audit approaches and so on. By hiring an integrator, you are essentially attempting to mitigate project risk *without* giving up responsibility for the project.

The Potential Risk Associated with an Integrator

It might be surprising to think about the risks of using an integrator but these need to be thought through and planned for as well. These risks include the following:

Wrong Staff Applied to your Project

Perhaps the integrator is busy with a variety of projects and doesn't have a deep bench? Making sure that your project gets the right staff from the integrator to do the job is very important. Their project team is supposed to bring additional expertise and experience to the project but if you are supplied with junior resources or inexperienced resources, then the integrator will add nothing and may even worsen overall project risk. As importantly is that the staff they provide need to fit culturally into your organization. A project manager who is too abrasive or simply doesn't get along with other staff on the project can do more harm than good. Therefore, ensuring that the integrator provides the right team at the right time is something that needs to be managed through the project.

No Incentive to Complete the Project

Depending on how the integration firm is compensated for their assistance there may not be an incentive for them to complete the project in the time scales desired. While this is unusual, it can occur if the integrator is paid on a time and materials basis and the project lacks strong direction from the company procuring the software. In essence, the project will still require strong internal project management and steering.

A Word about the Use of Consultants in Software Selection

When commenting upon potential risks in using external consultants and integrators, we should also cover the actual software selection project. Consultants are often used in assisting with software selection projects and rightly so for the reasons outlined above. However, the buyer should also be aware of the following issues;

Use of template Request for Proposal documents – an external consultant will most likely have developed a template for an RFP in which most common requirements are already stated and the majority of the document is in place. The idea is to save time by using the pre-built template and editing it to suit the current client. While new requirements are often added to the template to create a specific RFP, the contents should also be examined to REMOVE any requirements hat are not needed that are included in the template. Not removing unwanted requirements can result in an over engineered and hence more expensive and complex solution than is really required.

Selection bias – it is not uncommon for software consultancies and integration firms to have developed close relationships with the vendors that they routinely work with either formally via some form of alliance or informally via a close working relationship. While this can be useful it can also potentially result in bias towards a particular vendor/product. Buyers of software should examine the record of selections by a consultant/integrator prior to hiring them to see if a pattern of bias exists. This bias might be obvious in the sense that the consultant has a preponderance to select a certain product over and over but it may also be somewhat unobvious represented as a template RFP document which inadvertently favors a certain product too. This needs to be guarded against.

Summary

The use of third-party consultants and integrators is a common feature of ETRM software selection and implementation projects. Their use can be advantageous in reducing project risks and in the introduction of expertise and methodologies into the project. However, in selecting a third-party integrator/consultant, the buyer should also recognize the potential pitfalls too.

CHAPTER 12

THE IMPORTANCE OF TESTING

"Last But Not Least" Before Go-Live

Mr. Roger Schaffland,

Deloitte & Touche LLP

1.0 Introduction

One of the most overlooked and underperforming aspects we have found in Energy Trading/Risk Management (ETRM) system implementation projects is the testing phase, yet it's one of the most crucial aspects of the implementation. Many otherwise successful projects have dashed themselves on the rocks of a poorly planned/executed test process and have failed to deliver a reliable and full featured system in a timely manner as a result. Numerous companies "don't know what they don't know" about testing and incorrectly assume that the implementers or their own people have good/adequate testing skills. This chapter won't teach you everything about testing for ETRM implementation, but it should start you thinking about the critical parts and what kind of planning you need for proper testing.

Many projects treat testing as an afterthought, something that happens just before go-live, is conducted by the developers and/or vendors, and can be completed in two to four weeks regardless of system complexity. Wrong, painfully wrong. Thinking that way will always result in poorly planned/executed testing.

Poorly planned and/or executed testing (which happens too often in this author's opinion) increases project risk, usually raises the overall project cost, could result in the rejection of the system, and ultimately hurt the business case for implementation. Conversely, well planned/executed testing reduces project risk and installs confidence in the process to implement the system.

The upside is very good; the downside is very bad – so why don't project managers like testing? Because it takes work – both preparation and vigilance – and there are very few examples of well planned and executed testing to follow. Leaving it to chance and a prayer is never a good business model.

Testing takes time, skilled resources, advanced planning, and discipline; no ETRM system goes in right without all of these in good proportion. The typical cascading consequences of poorly planned/executed testing are shown in Figure 1.1.

Figure 1.1: Possible Consequences of Poorly Planned Testing

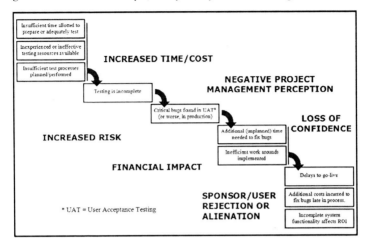

1.1 Most Common Problems

In the course of this chapter, we will share with you ways to avoid the top five reasons for testing problems as listed below:

- Insufficient planning/preparation

- Insufficient test window/test time in project plan

- Lack of defined requirements to properly structure tests/test processes

- Lack of proper testing processes/tools

- Lack of an experienced testing manager leading the planning and execution

Thus it follows that among the many challenges for an ETRM project is how to properly estimate the amount of time and effort to install in your overall project plan so that testing costs, when to start testing and who should be involved are anticipated. Your testing competence is a factor in this planning effort; most organizations do not have good/sufficient competency for testing.

> **Tip #1:** *Assess your testing competency for a system implementation project before you begin.*
>
> *Testing capability should be considered separately from the development and implementation competency of your team. Before you begin your implementation, check to see if you/your team have <u>recent</u>, successful testing experience with the same class of applications in a similar environment to this project. To be successful, you should find:*
>
> - *Tools*
> - *Applicable test cases/scenarios*
> - *Lessons learned documentation*
> - *Well defined processes*
> - *Report templates*
> - *Available resources with prior testing experience*
>
> *Many companies don't find all of these things and look to an implementation partner or vendor to help them with testing activities; this can also be an economical way to learn good testing behavior for future use if the project conducts a testing skill transfer as*

2.0 Proper Test Planning

2.1 Types of Testing

The recommended testing phases for a commercial ETRM system implementation with which your team should have competency include:

- Unit Testing (reports and custom software elements)
- System Testing (includes Performance Testing, Stress Testing, and Security Testing)
- Integration Testing (interfaces between separate system components and other applications)
- Quality Assurance Testing (ongoing testing in an environment that mirrors production)
- User Acceptance Testing (testing conducted by real users of the system, just before go-live)

Note: There are two special classes of testing called "Regression Testing" and "Post Implementation Monitoring" that will not be discussed in this chapter, but information on how to plan and manage these testing activities is separately available from Deloitte & Touche upon request.

Figure 2.1 shows some rough estimates of how much time to "split" between testing activities, but each project's testing time varies based on type of implementation (see Table 2.1 for the typical groupings, and from that table. Figure 2.1 is more typical of a Type II (Typical) implementation). An experienced test manager can put approximate times in place based on the type of implementation; use these estimates to cross check the validity of your project plan to make user your project isn't underestimating the test time needed.

Figure 2.1 Test Time Estimates as a Percent of Overall Test Time (Type II: Typical)

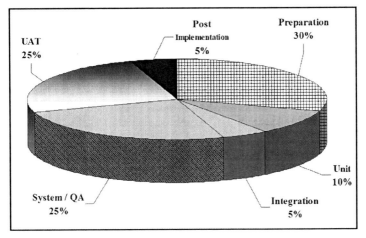

2.2 Cost Estimating

As we've just seen in Figure 1.0, the costs of poorly planned testing are enormous and the consequences far outweigh what anyone would budget for test activities; however, there are some basic costs associated with testing that every ETRM implementation project plan should include. If we divide the typical ETRM implementations into four basic types (light, typical, big, and custom), we can provide some cost modeling inputs for your project (note: these are only suggestions):

Table 2.1 Test Planning Inputs By Implementation Type

	Type I (LIGHT)	Type II (TYPICAL)	Type III (BIG)	Type IV (CUSTOM)
Project Characteristics				
A. Commercial ETRM System Used	Yes	Yes	Yes	No
B. Configuration Effort Expected	Light	Medium	Heavy	Heavy
C. Integration Effort Expected	None	Some	Significant	Significant
D. Implementation Time Estimate	6-12 months	8-18 months	12-24months	Variable
E. Custom Modules/Reports	No	Yes	Yes	Yes
Suggested Time, Tools & Resources				
1. Time: Unit Test Time (min)	1-2 weeks	2-4 weeks	4-6 weeks	Variable
2. Time: System Test Time (min)	4 weeks	4-8 weeks	8-10 weeks	Variable
3. Time: Integration Test Time (min)	None	2 weeks	> 4 weeks	Variable
4. Time: UAT Time (min)	2 weeks	2 weeks	2-4 weeks	Variable
5. Tools: Bug Tracking Tool	Yes	Yes	Yes	Yes
6. Tools: Source Code Library	Not Typical	Maybe	Yes	Yes
7. Tools: Test Case Management	Not Typical	Maybe	Yes	Yes
8. Tools: Automated Testing Tools	No	No	Maybe	Yes
9. Tools: Test Scenarios	Yes/Light	Yes	Yes	Yes
10. Resource: Testing Manager	Part Time	Part Time	Full Time	Full Time
11. Resource: Testers	Yes	Yes	Yes	Yes
12. Resource: QA Technician	Not Typical	Maybe	Yes	Yes

Notes: 1. Time estimates vary by vendor and many other factors, use these categories as a guideline and way to introduce a "multiplier" into your planning

2.3 Multiple Test Environments

To properly conduct testing, the system administrators in your company will need to create several separately managed environments. Each environment will likely have different copies of data and different versions of the ETRM system pointing to them. It can get complicated and introduce an unexpectedly heavy workload on technical support staff if you don't plan for this upfront; it can be a critical failure point in your implementation process to have uncertainty (and lack of access to qualified resources) in your support process around testing. The environments typically created to support ETRM implementation are:

* SANDBOX   * TRAIN

* DEVELOPMENT (DEV) * QUALITY ASSURANCE (QA)

* TEST   * PRODUCTION (PROD)

Tip #2: Make sure you have enough software licenses for multiple environments.

As part of your purchasing activities, make sure that your ETRM vendor understands your licensing needs for multiple environments. It can be a very low cost to add additional environments like DEV, TEST, QA, TRAIN, etc to your PROD license if you set this up BEFORE you sign your initial agreement. If you look for additional licenses after your initial purchase, you will likely pay much higher than you should.

Also, make sure you include your disaster recovery site license in your negotiations. For more information on tips for software licensing, ask Deloitte & Touche for a copy of our ETRM whitepaper: ***"Lessons Learned for SW Contracting."***

Each of the environments has a set of expectations for support and owner control and typically represent a chain of confidence from unsupported environments all the way to the official production environment. Note: TRAIN does not typically have a testing function.

Objects (code, configuration files, etc.) are often migrated out of each environment and into a source code control library for central storage before being promoted (upward) into the next environment, or sometimes, an entire environment can be overwritten by a separate environment, usually in a downward process as is shown in the figure below. What should be obvious from the figure is how much data transport and interrelationship there is between environments; it is a significant part of the system administrator's responsibilities to manage the data "refreshing" and permissions within each environment

Figure 2.2 Environment Interrelationships

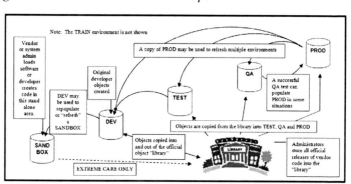

Tip #3: Change user names and integration points between environments

One of the most serious challenges in a sophisticated ETRM environment is making sure users are logging into the correct environment for the intended purpose. It can cause disaster to have a tester logging into production without realizing it, or having a non-production system update a production integrated system, or having a production user waste time in a non-production environment. To ensure that the environments are separate, the system administrators should create and maintain separate userids and clear definitions of integration system names in each environment.

For example, as part of the copy of PROD into any other environment, never duplicate real userids, instead use TEST_TRADER,QA_BACKOFFICE, DEV_RISKMGR, etc. Also, the administrators should follow the same setup guidance in integrated systems, so that it should be impossible for a TEST_TRADER to connect to a real PROD integration point using that login.

SANDBOX: As the name suggests, a sandbox is a personal "scratch area" where an individual or small group of individuals may keep a very local view of code, applications, data and relaxed permissions for development/demo/training use. These are important to set up, because it lets these individuals work quickly without a lot of administrative overhead. Vendors may use these spaces for pre-release code, demos, or unit testing activities using local configuration information. Developers may use these areas as personal copies for individual development. Accordingly, these environments quickly become "polluted" with custom configurations, unsupported code releases, etc. and will require numerous "refreshes" from the "master" source code and data. Never allow code or any other type of object to be migrated from Sandbox to the source code library or any other environment without extra scrutiny. Sandboxes are refreshed at the request of the owner. Try not to let too many Sandbox environments spring up, because they add significant burden to the system administrator overhead (refreshing and fixing) and undermine the need to use the official DEV environment.

DEV: The development area is usually a copy of the TEST or PROD environment and is where developers should do most of their serious development and unit testing. Objects are copied into and out of the source code library. DEV is usually refreshed when a new official version of TEST is established, but it can happen that a new official release of PROD refreshes multiple environments including DEV. DEV should generally be the same ETRM software code release level as the TEST environment.

TEST: TEST is the environment where system and integration testing should be performed (usually by a combination of project support and production users). TEST is usually refreshed from PROD with officially released objects from the source code library installed and is where new releases of the ETRM code are initially reviewed. TEST is often at a later release date than PROD or QA. The hardware in TEST is not usually as robust as is used in QA or PROD.

QA: The QA environment should be almost identical (hardware and software) to the PROD environment (with different userids and system integration points from PROD, see Tip #3) and is where any patches (from developers or vendors) are tested (preferably by production users) before they are released to the production environment. In addition to the limited system testing related to each patch, the overall ETRM system should undergo regression testing to see if any other adverse effects are noticed. The need and scope for regression testing increases with the scope of patch or size/importance of vendor software update. This can result in an extreme amount of effort and is why most companies do not upgrade ETRM versions as often as vendors issue releases. User Acceptance Testing is usually conducted in QA before project go-live and in these rare circumstances, QA is usually used to generate PROD. If QA is identical to PROD (hardware and software), then performance testing (a form of system testing) can occur in the QA environment.

PROD: The only kind of testing that usually occurs in PROD is performance monitoring. Performance monitoring is not covered in this chapter.

The typical sets of environments and their testing uses are shown in Figure 2.3.

Figure 2.3 Multiple Environments for Testing

TEST TYPE	Widget 4.0 Alpha Patches None (SANDBOX)	Widget 3.2 Patches, X, Y, Z (DEV)	Widget 3.2 Patches X, Y (TEST)	Widget 3.1 Patches A, B, C (QA)	Widget 3.1 Patches A, B (PROD)
UNIT	X	X			
INTEGRATION			X		
SYSTEM			X	X	
USER ACCEPTANCE				X	
REGRESSION				X	
PRODUCTION MONITORING					X

2.4 Resources

Referencing the information in Table 2.1 we'll describe some further thoughts about the recommended resources for testing:

THE TESTING MANAGER

As identified in section 1.1 The Most Common Problems, not having an experienced test manager to lead the planning and execution of testing is a typical failure point for most ETRM implementations. In almost all of the implementation types in Figure 2.1, we recommend a part time or full time role for a testing manager and a test team to support him/her. Most companies try to identify a resource from inside the project, but it is critical to find a candidate who actually has previous, SUCCESSFUL, experience implementing a major technical system, preferably at that company (or equivalent system experience). If you can't find one inside your team, then look more broadly within your company or even in the user base for the vendor application you are implementing and also in the consulting field among experienced ETRM implementers.

Question: If you had the pick of two candidates, both with experience testing and implementing an ETRM system (or similar application), who would make the best testing manager, a deep technical expert or a strong business analyst/manager?

Answer: In our opinion, **a strong business analyst/manager is the better choice for a testing manager.** The reason is simple, when it comes to push vs. shove (and there will be both at the critical juncture of testing toward implementation), it will be most critical to have someone making decisions with the support and backing of the business community. Knowing "what should be tested and why", is more important than "what is possible to test and how." A technical testing manager is a very good resource, but we suggest that a crucial find is a strong business contact who will champion and defend a testing plan that best supports the business needs.

TESTERS

The number of testers depends on the size of the project and the type of implementation and timeline, but they should be dedicated to their testing tasks and not have other responsibilities (especially not development/configuration efforts).

Tip #4: Testing requires an independent perspective.

Except for unit testing, it is a conflict of interest to have the implementers or vendors conduct their own testing. For best results, the implementation project is best served by a team of independent testers with relevant competence in the system and business processes. Often this is the client team during UAT, but it is more efficient to have this take place with a combination of client people and consultants before UAT.

There is also an expectation that testers will be detailed oriented and able to follow a rigid process so that the testing activities themselves are thorough and well documented. However, it is possible to have too much process and too much testing focus; some authors have even referred to it as the need to have "good enough" testing instead of perfection. There will be a point at which the testing manager must decide to accept the number of bugs, work arounds, and enhancement requests and decide to move the system into the hands of the real business users for their expert judgment and bug classification.

Tip #5: The best testers are the client's own people.

There is a curve of diminishing returns related to testing by non-client personnel. Client testing often reveals features, configuration elements and changes to business processes that are logical to the vendor/implementer but not to the client personnel. Use the 80/20 rule to decide when to include the client's actual representatives in testing. New bugs and new prioritizations are bound to come from this switch in testing resources.

QA TECHNICIAN

In very large, or custom developed, ETRM implementation projects, there can also be a role for a Quality Assurance (QA) Technician, which is a very different role from a tester. This is a specialized role to interface between the results of testing efforts and the formal promotion of code to QA or PROD environments, especially when it's a very complex environment or system. Primarily, QA Technicians conduct additional tests to make sure the identified programs/objects perform according to documented parameters and work to ensure PROD is not affected by any gaps in testing. QA Technician testing includes both new objects and updated or modified versions of existing objects. Some of the QA Technician's specific duties include:

- Reviews release documentation for completeness and adherence to defined processes
- Creates/maintains documentation of test release procedures
- Works with the Testing Manager(s) to coordinate/batch together code releases
- Works with DBAs to maintain deployment environment integrity
- Performs/completes release procedures
- Creates reports / logs issues pertaining to releases
- Reviews operating parameters of deployment environments during and after code releases

- Coordinates environment downtime and availability with users and support teams
- Communicates with management and deployment teams about results of reviews and testing

2.5 Testing Workload Planning

One of the biggest issues we see is a lack of a broader view of the testing stream management from the beginning of the project through the actual test execution. Most project managers don't consider that test planning can and should start in the early planning stages of the project and fail to recognize that a Testing Manager has inputs to and deliverables in all phases of a project. Figure 2.4 illustrates the workload.

Figure 2.4 Testing Activities and Relative Workload by Phase

PLAN	DESIGN	DEVELOP	TEST	IMPLEMENT
• Create test plan • Define testing roles/responsibilities • Identify testing resources • Identify tools • Evaluate testing competency • Develop budget requirements • Define testing protocols for remote testers (if applicable) **DELIVERABLES** • Test plan • Updated project plan • Remote testing protocols	• Review requirements • Estimate test time • Create UAT plan • Define test environment including "Sandbox" • Install/configure source code control tools **DELIVERABLES** • UAT plan • Updated project plan • Test scenarios	• Install/configure "sandbox" env.. • Conduct unit testing • Review test metrics • Update test allocation based on review of updated requirements • Install and configure test and acceptance test environment • Create system and integration test plans **DELIVERABLES** • Unit test results • Updated test scenarios • Updated project plan • Integration test plan • System test plan	• Populate test environments • Conduct integration test • Conduct system test • Conduct quality assurance test • Review test metrics **DELIVERABLES** • Test results • Updated project plan • Bug log	• Conduct User Acceptance test (UAT) • Support users during testing • Create "post roll-out" monitoring plan **DELIVERABLES** • UAT test results • Updated bug log • Monitoring plan ■ = unit of work

2.6 Financial Considerations in Testing

The business case for proper testing is very clear; the earlier you can fix something in the process to promote software to production the less it costs to do so. It should come as no surprise that fixing bugs in a unit test, when the problem is smaller or more localized, is better and more economical than in fixing that same bug during User Acceptance Testing or after go-live when business activities or Go-Live may be impacted.

Also, if there is a commercial vendor package involved, buyers should tie the final vendor payment to the proper testing scope and successful bug-fixing as a function of acceptance before production go-live; this gives extra incentive for the vendor to complete testing under the original implementation contract. Post Go-Live testing by a vendor will always cost more and will come with a different set of deadline expectations. The worst case scenario is that uncaught bugs may not get fixed until much later in the project implementation and affect the ROI and business case that supports the overall implementation.

3.0 Test Methodology

3.1 Requirements for Testing

Every good project has checks and balances. Testing is the natural check that requirements are done properly and have been achieved during the implementation. Therefore requirements definition is the most fundamental aspect of your implementation, including testing – without requirements there is no testing need and no logical way to "accept" the system.

Tip #6: Work from a signed off list of comprehensive business and technical requirements.

The test planning process should start with the evaluation of the requirements process. You should expect your project to continually refine the testing scope as the project proceeds toward implementation; however, fundamental changes in requirements can impair test planning. Ask these four questions in the early stages of the project:

A) Did/will the requirements development go through a robust evaluation and prioritization process including a final review by business and technical analysts?

B) Are the requirements endorsed by the business sponsor and relevant implementation partner(s)?

C) Did the evaluation of requirements include a segmentation into elements that are "configuration" versus "custom develop or integration" requirements? (see Section 2.4 for why this is important)

D) Is there a defined "scope change" process that includes reassessment of testing effort?

Most ETRM implementations do not use pure Rapid Application Design (RAD) or AGILE development methodology, so it is more likely your project will use at least a portion of traditional "waterfall" approach. Your ability to know the largest portion, and most complex set, of high priority requirements as early as possible is critical to your ability to plan and allocate time to the various phases, including testing. It is important for the Testing Manager to be close to the process of changing requirements and have the ability to assess the impacts of these changes on all aspects of the testing process including time allocation and structure of the UAT process.

3.2 Elements of a Test Plan

Another element of the planning and preparation is to set down some operating procedures with your steering committee and user group. Create a test plan document and gain specific acceptance for that document with the steering committee and the business owner. The plan should describe the types of testing to be performed and the testing protocols to be used. (Deloitte & Touche has boilerplate material you can use for this) The benefit of this process is that it formally defines the activities and timelines for participation which sets the expectations early in the project for both business and technical personnel.

A written test plan document created and agreed to early in the project that covers the following points will help business and project sponsors to understand the effort and foresight needed to contribute to testing preparation/execution.

- Scope of testing activities
- Roles and responsibilities
- Methodology
- Acceptance criteria
- Resource requirements
- Tools and templates
- Appendix A: The test project plan

The actual test scenarios are a separate deliverable from the test plan and should be constructed early but evolve as requirements are defined and actual development is completed. If your organization or implementation partner has good testing competence (see Tip #1) these may already be available for your business and commodity type.

161

Tip #7: Evaluate how much of the system you are testing as part of formal "ACCEPTANCE"

It is quite possible to have a detailed test plan together with a robust set of testing activities and ultimately decide to accept a system but only test a minor share of the system. Often times, clients do not test the standard components of an incoming ETRM system, preferring to focus on the complex custom development areas. This can have the effect of not fully exploring configuration before go-live and result in embarrassing post go-live "gotchas". Also, some clients accept systems with modules that they have paid for, but do not have any immediate need for; it is an oversight to not address this as part of testing before go-live.

We recommend that a standard set of tests for each major module of an incoming ETRM system be added to the testing scenarios. They don't have to be high priority, but should be completed as part of good due diligence. It helps to set the expectation with the vendor that the entire system is configured and ready to produce valid outputs. Rely on consultants to pull standard test scenarios together if needed.

3.3   Severity Levels

Establishing a <u>simple</u> set of agreed upon severity levels for reported bugs is a fundamental need of every testing project. Making them too complex or providing too many levels will bog down your bug reporting. We recommend that you strive to make the reporting fit the simple four level system depicted in table 3.1. You will notice that the focus is on deciding which bugs will impact the Go-Live process (Day 1). Testing managers should ensure that testing eliminates all S1 (Critical) bugs before delivering the system into production. The primary effort before Go-Live should be to resolve all open S1 bugs or have the bug owners (and business users) adjust to S1 bugs to S2 bugs in the weeks before Go-Live or the Go-Live schedule will need to be pushed back.

Table 3.1 Bug Severity Reference Table

Severity Level	Description
S0 (Closed)	Bugs or issues that have been resolved or closed and do not require further work effort.
S1 (Critical)	Must be fixed prior to Go-Live or the system will not operate properly on Day 1 and no viable workaround is available.
S2 (Severe)	Should be fixed as soon as possible because the problem will impact the system on Day 1, but a viable workaround exists to allow for Go-Live to proceed.
S3 (Minor)	Should be fixed at some point, but the problem will not impact the system on Day 1.
S4 (Enhancement)	Probably does not need to be fixed. This is a "Nice to have" change.

Tip #8: *Bug owners set the bug severity level*

During testing, it is essential to establish who the owner of a bug is. That owner (business or technical) sets the severity of the bug and works cooperatively with the implementation team and testing manager to resolve or create work arounds for reported bugs. The best policy is to ensure that the bug owner is the only person who can lower the bug rating to a less critical level. The testing manager should work with bug owners to agree on the severity/criticality of reported bugs.

3.4 Test Planning Using the "V-Model"

Test planning should commence during the early phases of the implementation. Activities such as developing quality criteria and test plans can parallel the implementation as it moves from planning/scoping through design, development and implementation. This has the added benefit of providing more upfront planning consideration for testing than waiting until the crunch time of go-live planning. The Deloitte & Touche recommended approach (and best suited for "waterfall" type implementations) is the V-Model, which can be seen below. This model is based upon standard energy trading scenarios that describe the usual and "to-be" front, middle, and back office technical and operational elements of an ETRM implementation.

Figure 3.1 The V-Model

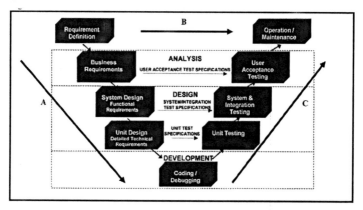

The V-Model demonstrates how the User Acceptance Test process (typically one of the last activities before go-live) is, in fact, one of the first elements that can/should be scoped and planned, since its specifications come from the Business Requirements effort. Traversing down the left most leg of the "V" provides increasingly greater clarity on the design and configuration of the ETRM system and traversing up the right leg of the "V" is the order of test execution for the successful delivery of the system. As each step on the left is complete, your project should start to plan and design the associated test process on the right. Once your project reaches the bottom of the "V" you can start to create detailed (or more optimally, modify/update) the test cases/processes you have already planned.

If done properly, you will have written/planned a significant portion of your UAT process before you have started to write code or started configuring your system. This is probably the most important change in project thinking around testing – it should start up front, right at the early stages of your project.

Tip #9: Watch out for cascading "phase failure".

Many ETRM implementation projects "try their best" to fit in all the last minute requirements and bug fixes and wind up with very little time to adequately test the application before Go-Live. You can spot these projects because each phase of the project starts to slip into the next phase, and unwise project managers allow scope creep to consume the contingency time built into most projects without extending the testing start time or duration. Suddenly, testing start times are also being asked to delay and testing time must shorten in order to make the project's Go-Live date remain the same. This is cascading phase failure, don't enable this to hit your project.

Instead the testing manager should spot that the plan, design, and develop phases are increasingly becoming longer because scope creep is affecting on-time delivery for each phase. The testing manager should identify that the testing phase could be at risk and properly defend the timely use of agreed upon resources (people, test suites, systems, etc.) plus logical time estimates and re-emphasize the need for a complete and proper test cycle.

4.0 Tools & Processes

As a general rule, we do not recommend introducing new tools and process complexity as part of an implementation. Most implementations are time sensitive and new tools are usually a burden on a tight plan. If you do introduce new tools, be sure to leverage experienced resources from within your company or in the consulting space to help you use them to the best outcome.

4.1 Automated Testing Tools

Energy clients are starting to develop automated testing suites using commercial packages such as those from HP/Mercury™ but there are a few "lessons learned" about starting and maintaining this effort. If done properly, automated testing can reduce weeks of manual testing effort to an overnight run, but be aware of these issues:

- Multiple vendor packages may be needed and the costs are significant

- Lengthy configuration cycles (4-8 months x 1-2 people) are required to create a useful testing suite

- Automated testing is best suited to those tasks for which the expected result is a known value, such as in testing of risk management results

- Automated testing does need an initial investment of time from business users to help configure and set up the tests and document results

- Automated testing suites need continual maintenance to keep pace with code releases and custom development; the ROI for automated testing goes away quickly if the suite becomes out of date from PROD software configuration

The benefits of automated testing are primarily the shortened amount of time to get results with less involvement of the business users, combined with consistent testing actions and the ability to return feedback to developers/implementers faster. The ROI for automated testing is best realized when several large testing cycles can be run using the same test suite without significant modification. One client used the same automated testing suite for both a major ETRM software upgrade and then again to support a switch from Sybase to Oracle on that same ETRM version and saved significant amounts of time and effort testing the results of the operations.

4.2 Bug Reports

Every implementation encounters bugs and enhancement requests. Likewise, every project should have a simple, secure, multi-user tool that is widely available to record bugs and generate reports. Projects can use any variety of commercial tools or something home-grown in Excel™ or Access™. Upon request, Deloitte & Touche will provide such tools to interested clients for integrated detailed bug reporting and summary reporting. Some screen snapshots are provided here.

Figure 4.1 Sample Tools/Reports for Bug Reporting

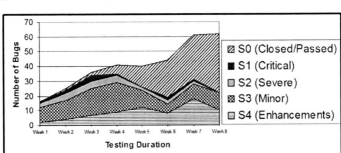

TYPICAL FEATURES
- MS Access based
- Multi-user
- Email notification enabled
- Fast data entry
- Calendar based logic
- Customizable by client/project
- Integrated with change management
- Provides both summary and detail bug reports

DETAILED BUG REPORT

SUMMARY BUG REPORT

Bug Tracking and Change Log Tool

4.3 Bug logs

In your project, you should be able to produce a log of the errors found during testing from the tool used to record bugs. The frequency of bug reporting depends on the type of testing being conducted. It is generally acceptable to produce bug reports weekly to support project review meetings, but during UAT, the frequency could be daily. Looking at the number and rate of increase or decrease of Critical or Severe bugs (see Table 3.1) is a critical activity during testing. An example of a graphical way to display this information can be seen in figure 4.2.

Figure 4.2 Sample Bug Log Overview (System Test)

Legend:
- S0 (Closed/Passed)
- S1 (Critical)
- S2 (Severe)
- S3 (Minor)
- S4 (Enhancements)

Y-axis: Number of Bugs (0–70)
X-axis: Testing Duration (Week 1 – Week 8)

Figure 4.2 displays a typical "hump" that most testing managers will recognize in a system testing cycle. The first "hump" is due to the immediate surge of discovered bugs over several reporting periods followed by later software fixes that close those same bugs which explains the rise and the fall in the graph in Weeks 1-6 of this sample graphic. The second hump (Weeks 6-8) is typical after a major fix is implemented and regression testing finds new bugs or rediscovers old ones in different scenarios. The important trends to note in most bug reporting (easily seen in a graphical depiction such as Figure 4.2) are:

- The number of Critical bugs should not keep increasing, and should go to zero before go-live

- The amount of time that Critical bugs are open should be decreasing

- The number of Severe bugs should also be decreasing over time

- The number of Closed/Passed bugs should be increasing steadily

There are many types of reports that are useful to help with testing processes, your choice of bug reporting tools should have several options for you to use with minimal configuration/setup.

Offshore Testing

A quick thought about offshore testing efforts. In multiple surveys of our client base, we have yet to find a firm example of significant savings delivered from the use of offshore testing resources for ETRM implementation. Early indications of cheap labor and experienced resources have been replaced by anecdotal stories of poor quality and significantly more overhead to manage and maintain testing processes. We are still looking for good case studies to prove how to best conduct offshore testing for ETRM implementations, so please contact us if you think you have a good approach.

Conclusion

Of all the activities that contribute to ETRM implementation success, testing is probably the last great frontier and one of the areas that can significantly improve with relatively minor investments and adjustments in project planning. Primary among all the recommendations in this chapter is to accurately gauge your testing competence (see Tip #1) before undertaking ETRM implementation and to work with partners if necessary to improve your company's testing methodology. These will really help improve your chances of successful implementation. The risks are high and the costs are too great not to improve the basics like test planning in every phase and identifying "cascading phase failure" before it's too late.

Disclaimer

of performance or quality. Deloitte Touche Tohmatsu expressly disclaims all implied warranties, including, without limitation, warranties of merchantability, title, fitness for a particular purpose, noninfringement, compatibility, security, and accuracy.

Your use of these materials and information contained therein is at your own risk, and you assume full responsibility and risk of loss resulting from the use thereof. Deloitte Touche Tohmatsu will not be liable for any special, indirect, incidental, consequential, or punitive damages or any other damages whatsoever, whether in an action of contract, statute, tort (including, without limitation, negligence), or otherwise, relating to the use of these materials or the information contained therein.

If any of the foregoing is not fully enforceable for any reason, the remainder shall nonetheless continue to apply.

SECTION 4

MAINTAINING YOUR ETRM SYSTEM

CHAPTER 13

SUPPORT & MAINTENANCE AGREEMENTS

Dr. Gary M. Vasey,

UtiliPoint International, Inc.

Once the software is installed, the support & maintenance agreement and your chosen vendor's ability to honor it will become extremely important. The Support & Maintenance agreement will cost in the region of 15-25% of the license fees that were paid for the software – typically 20% annually. It should cover standard upgrades and issue resolution at least so long as the software being used is a recent version. Generally, the vendor's support & maintenance agreement will cover a number of versions – perhaps three – back from its current release and so it is wise to try to stay as current as possible with the vendor's release schedule.

The vendor's standard support & maintenance agreement should have been provided as part of the package of documentation reviewed during selection. It might also have been customized during the contract negotiations. It is an important document and should be properly understood by the person responsible for support onsite. As stated above, at a minimum, it should define terms for proper support of the vendor's software including being able to receive free upgrades to the software during the agreement period as well as what constitutes a software issue and how and who will resolve it and in what time scales.

Software Upgrades

Third-party ETRM software changes quite rapidly because the industry requirements can change quite quickly (new instruments, new rules, new regulations, and so on) but also because the vendor is often adding functionality to win new business, enter new niches in the industry and to keep its existing clients happy. It's not uncommon for a vendor to have between 4 and 6, even more in some instances, releases a year. These releases will also include fixes to reported bugs and software issues in addition to new functionality.

For the user, this rapid release of new versions of software can be quite onerous. Depending on how the vendor organizes the release schedule, there will be major releases – perhaps annually – that might include substantial changes in look and feel, architecture, configuration and larges tranches of new functionality, and minor releases – generally bug fix releases. Since the user is obliged to stay up with the vendor's release schedule as per the support & maintenance agreement, it can mean a lot of work.

In the past, software quality has also been an issue in the ETRM software category. In part, the rapid changes in functionality and, in part, the fact that many ETRM vendors were quite small and resource constrained meant that the vendor's software testing was sometimes inadequate. Users loath to introduce new bugs and issues into their business environment were therefore often reluctant to stay apace with the vendor and could often fall many releases behind. So far behind in fact, that support issues arose. Since the support & maintenance agreement states how many versions behind the current release the vendor will, in fact, support, users often found themselves paying for custom support for their software version even though a support &

maintenance agreement was in place. In recent years, the overall quality of ETRM software has improved considerably. None the less, such issues can still arise if the user falls behind too far.

The user however must maintain a number of software environments in addition to the live environment in order to test upgrades issued by the vendor. Not to test an upgrade is foolish no matter how hard the vendor worked on testing simply because there are aspects of each user's business and how the software is used that are unique and simply cannot be adequately tested by the vendor.

Maintaining a live and numerous test environments can be quite costly in hardware terms but in fact the need to be constantly testing new software versions can also be costly in people terms. It requires data and users to check that the software works as advertised and continues to meet the needs of the business. These costs are often forgotten by buyers of the software but they should be factored in and understood when budgeting to procure ETRM software.

Another issue that needs to be understood is the position of custom software written specifically for the user or, indeed by the user, perhaps to interface the ETRM software with other software in the enterprise. In the latter case, it is unlikely that it is covered by any support arrangement with the vendor and so will need to be maintained internally adding further cost. In the former case, it is wise to check if custom software is covered or not. Additional support fees might be required in order to have the vendor support that custom software it delivered. The real issue with custom software components though is whether subsequent upgrades from the vendor will still integrate with the custom software? This is an issue that must be discussed with the vendor.

Even though the support and maintenance agreement will likely cover free software upgrades from the vendor, the user should consider the expenses associated with keeping up with the vendor's release program and the possible consequences of falling behind.

Issue Resolution

The support & maintenance agreement will also define how support will be delivered by the vendor. In general, software issues will be classified according to their severity and the support & maintenance agreement will define those classifications and the criteria for their resolution. Most usually, the agreement will allow for issues to be classed as 'critical' requiring immediate resolution (perhaps in a 24 hour period), 'severe' requiring resolution over a longer period and 'routine' where resolution can be over an extended period. The agreement will also identify procedures for reporting issues to the vendor and will define what types of issues are actually covered by the agreement. In the case of the latter point, software issues that turn out to have been caused by inappropriate use of the software by the user in any way will almost certainly not be covered under the agreement. The agreement will most likely also define the process for making enhancement requests to the vendor.

A critical software issue is one that essentially stops the user from conducting its business and is highly disruptive. It requires immediate resolution on the part of the vendor and the criteria for the definition of such issues should be defined in the agreement.

In reporting a software issue the user will utilize the process defined in the agreement. Most usually, the user will need to submit details regarding the characteristics of the issue along with error message printouts, data printouts and sufficient information for the vendor to attempt to recreate the issue. The vendor will acknowledge the receipt of the bug and assign it an identifier and severity rating hence communicating expectations regarding resolution timescales. Periodically, the vendor will also report on all issues that it working on for the user including the current status of the issue and how the fix is to be delivered. In some instances, more information might be requested by the vendor and, in some instances, the vendor might require access to the user's system to recreate the issue.

Quite often the vendor will determine that the issue is in fact a 'system feature' or 'user error. ETRM software is both complex and powerful software such that users can sometimes create an issue where in fact there isn't one. Too many 'user error' type issues reported by the user will undoubtedly trigger a proposal by the vendor to have the users undertake more training. Sometimes what appears to be a software issue is simply the software working as designed and this can trigger a decision on whether or not to make an enhancement request to modify the software (see below).

While critical issues will be dealt with as quickly as possible other non-critical issues and software bugs will be fixed by the vendor and included in a later software release as either a 'bug-fix' release or as part of a planned upgrade.

As suggested above, some reported issues might trigger additional fees especially if the issue was caused by user error such as direct and inappropriate manipulation of the database. Since the issue was caused by the user, the fix will be charged at support rates specified in the support & maintenance agreement.

Enhancement Requests

Some reported issues will become enhancement requests. Again, the vendor's support & maintenance agreement should specify a procedure for creating enhancement requests and how they are to be processed by the user and the vendor. The most usual procedure will involve both the vendor and user agreeing that that an enhancement is required followed by a definition and ranking of the enhancement request. Similar to issue reporting, enhancements will be prioritized according to some defined criteria.

The next step will likely be a quotation from the vendor for developing the enhancement followed by agreement and approval by the user. At that time, the specification will be developed and the enhancement scheduled for development and release by the vendor. Sometimes the support & maintenance agreement may include some limited scope for free enhancements – often not. In some instances, the vendor might deem the enhancement critical to its product, have already scheduled such an enhancement or have requests from other users for the same enhancement. In these instances, fees can be negotiated.

Sometimes, the vendor may have a User Group which, either by paying an annual fee or for free, it might allocate a number of development hours to. Common enhancements can often be channeled through a User Group to be considered as a part of any development hours the User Group has available.

Internal Support

The vendor's support & maintenance program may call for a procedure to be followed by the user that includes the use of internal support staff. In fact, this is a sensible and cost reducing approach since it stops users abusing the support system. Usually, internal support staff at the user's site is notified initially by their own users of issues, bugs and possible enhancements. The internal support staff will ensure that the issue isn't something related to the local environment, user error and so forth before reporting the issue to the vendor using the appropriate channels, processes and forms.

The use of internal support staff can ensure that additional fees are avoided and that users receive strong local support in their use of the software. Additionally, the user support staff can plan and execute upgrades, testing and training as well as ensure other items such as disaster backup and recovery services, support for custom software and interfaces and so on.

Summary

The support & maintenance agreement is a critical agreement that should be properly understood by the user but it is not a panacea. Proper support is expensive to deliver, requires dedicated staff and more. Providing proper support for ETRM software usually requires internal support staff and equipment to be budgeted for as well as the annual support & maintenance payment. Finally, the vendor will not support old versions of the software unless on a custom basis so it pays to stay up with the vendors release program.

CHAPTER 14

MANAGING UPGRADES - MITIGATING THE RISKS OF UPGRADING YOUR ETRM SYSTEMS

Angela Ryan, Director

&

Baris Ertan, Senior Manager,

The Structure Group

Comprehensive planning and goal setting will pay big dividends during and after the upgrade process

Aging legacy applications, a shift to asset-based trading, multi-commodity needs, a stricter controls environment and ongoing vendor/product consolidation are encouraging many energy companies to reevaluate their ETRM systems. Yet a number of organizations face a lack of understanding of their existing ETRM system capabilities, and in some cases, underutilization of system functionality and the potential of losing vendor support/maintenance are causing companies to fall behind on vendor upgrade schedules. Such companies are at a crossroads as they try to determine whether to upgrade to the latest version of their existing vendor package, procure a new vendor product or develop a custom solution.

There are several good ETRM applications available, yet finding the right combination of functionality, usability and compatibility with your organization's current information infrastructure can be a time- and resource-intensive process. Sarbanes-Oxley requirements further complicate this exercise as system and data integration become more crucial for compliance and reporting.

In addition, experience shows that the pain of a wrong decision can resonate for many years after deployment.

This article provides some guidance to those navigating this complex journey and draws upon the lessons The Structure Group has learned while partnering with clients to implement fully integrated ETRM systems.

Beginning the ETRM Upgrade Process

Beginning this process can be extremely overwhelming because it requires a comprehensive plan and solid end goal in mind. At Structure, we use the following methodology across our ETRM system implementations.

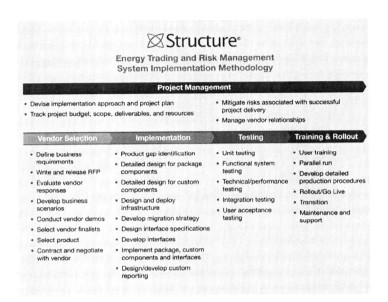

First and foremost, an ETRM-upgrade program begins with a thorough evaluation of both current and future business requirements. Based on these requirements, a gap analysis of existing system functionality can be conducted. Ideally, "build-versus-buy" decisions can be made with a detailed understanding of the business requirements and the current state of an organization's overall system infrastructure and internal IT development/support capability. Based on these alternatives, it is important to understand the advantages and disadvantages of each to determine the best approach given an acceptable level of cost, quality, time and delivery risk.

We have found that "build-versus-buy" decisions typically come down to whether a custom solution is sustainable and cost effective over time. Organizations pursuing custom ETRM solutions must ask themselves "Do we want to be in the software development business?" At Structure, we believe that custom solutions should be developed when the functional areas/system enablers are strategic, not tactical, to an organization's business. Another question to be asked is "Are our ETRM needs different from those of other energy companies?" In some unique situations, custom solutions do make sense. That said, we

181

believe there is a viable ETRM vendor marketplace that can meet many of the industry's requirements.

We generally advocate that custom software solutions focus on those areas of greatest competitive advantage, and that off-the-shelf packages be used elsewhere where possible. These bespoke elements can include the creation of custom pricing or optimization models or valuation tools for non-standard instruments.

In line with many software packages, the lifetime of an ETRM solution within an organization tends to average 5-6 years. Many organizations now have an older version of a current platform, and they face an interesting question.

On one hand, an upgrade to the latest version of the existing software can be far cheaper and quicker, although our experience shows that it is rarely the four-week exercise that some vendors may claim. On the other hand, a new implementation clearly offers many organizations far more potential benefits, including access to new technology and functionality and the chance to re-architect their ETRM solution to more closely reflect their current business activities. However, these new software implementations come at a cost.

There is also a middle ground. Some organizations are opting to "re-implement" the latest version of their existing platform by installing the latest version from scratch, rather than just doing the vendor-prescribed technical upgrade. This has many of the advantages that come with a new solution. Revisiting the configuration from scratch allows it to be closely aligned to the current business. Companies can leverage newer functionality in the package and remove obsolete data, reports and other functionality thereby helping to reduce support costs. In addition, the vendor is already known to the organization, internal support staff is familiar with the system, and the system's integration costs will generally be limited.

Vendor Selection

Choosing the right vendor product can be difficult, and there is no "silver bullet." Once business requirements have been defined, the next step is to evaluate vendor applications. When assessing ETRM applications, in addition to selecting a system that is the best functional fit, other key drivers influencing an organization's selection criteria should include:

- Proven Track Record
- Vendor Viability
- Product Viability
- Flexible Integration
- Performance
- Scalability
- Application Usability
- Vendor Support
- Ease of Implementation
- Configuration Flexibility
- Cost of Ownership

Request for Proposal: Although it is not always done, we believe it is important to issue a formal Request for Proposal (RFP). This helps ensure competitive pricing and allows vendors to address whether their system meets (or does not meet) the specific business requirements.

We recommend providing detailed business requirements to the vendors and asking them to provide responses to whether their system meets each requirement. Typically, vendors are allowed three responses:

- **Yes** – the functionality is fully supported with no customization or complex configuration required

- **Partial** – the functionality is partially supported by the software

- **No** – the functionality is not currently supported.

All vendor responses should be based on the capabilities of the current production release of software and not functionality that is currently in development or scheduled for a future release. It has become commonplace for these responses to be used when developing the software contract.

In addition to addressing business requirements, the RFP should also contain information related to:

- Technical requirements (architecture, integration, security, auditing, performance, etc.)
- Vendor Information (financials, company size, product history/future direction, install base)
- Pricing (license, maintenance, professional services)
- Implementation (methodology, project plan)
- References

Customer References: As part of the RFP process, the buyer should ask for the vendor to provide references from customers of similar size, complexity, trading activity, and asset mix. It is important for the buyer to contact these customers to understand the software's strengths and limitations and each customer's overall level of satisfaction. Furthermore, we also recommend conducting independent reference checks with customers not provided by the vendor during this process.

Vendor Demonstrations: Buyers should look beyond the basic ETRM functionality and instead focus on how the software handles more complex scenarios, especially those that are unique to the organization. To get the most out of these vendor demonstrations, the key step is to translate the buyer's business requirements into detailed business scenarios. This gives vendors the opportunity to incorporate these specific scenarios into their product to better showcase its capabilities.

During these demonstrations, it is important to be aware of overselling and vaporware. Buyers should ask to see everything demonstrated in the application and not settle for a screenshot or promises of future development. If vendors claim that certain functionality will be available in the next version, we recommend writing that into the contract, along with escape clauses should the functionality not work as required.

Vendor Scoring: A comprehensive scoring system should be formalized and clearly articulated. This ensures a high level of understanding of the selection criteria across all user groups. It is also critical to understand not only the capabilities of the selected product, but also its limitations. It is useful to conduct a gap assessment between the detailed requirements and the selected product's functionality to gauge the amount of work required to supplement the vendor implementation.

End users should be actively involved in the preparing demonstration scenarios and conducting vendor demonstrations. Each person should be encouraged to provide his or her independent scoring of the solution. A solution that only meets the needs of one or two groups will not be successful in the long run.

Once the results from the vendor RFP responses are compiled, customer reference checks, and demonstrations fully analyzed, the buyer should have all the data points and analysis to make the most informed and educated decision for the purchase of an ETRM system.

Contract Negotiations: Once a vendor has been chosen, the buyer will now be at the contract and negotiation stage. In our experience, it is not uncommon to not reach agreement with the initial vendor chosen. It is important to have another vendor to "fall back" on in negotiating terms and conditions of the contract. A 3rd party's involvement in this phase can be valuable to help evaluate vendor implementation commitment, definition of demonstrated capabilities, and functionality promised in future releases.

In the contract, the vendor should be very clear on the following:

- All modules that will be purchased. These should be tailed to buyer's needs.
- Costs – license, maintenance, and professional services
- Implementation Services – what the vendor will provide during implementation.
- Support Services – what the vendor will provide for support
- 3rd Party Software Fees (i.e., option models, integration tools, etc.)

Implementation

Project Planning: A strict project management discipline should be implemented to manage scope and meet delivery milestones. This includes developing detailed: project plan, project charter, scope definition, and project budget. In addition, clear communication should be established across all levels of the project team, along with well understood change control, status reporting and issues management procedures.

Product Design: Through our implementation experience, we have learned that it is important to use the ETRM product as a tool to facilitate design discussions right from the outset. The ability to influence design decisions is far higher in the earlier selection stages, and high levels of business-user engagement are essential. A common trap is for users to become engaged with the project only at the user-acceptance-testing stage or at "go-live" when it is already too late and expensive to make significant changes.

By involving all stakeholders early in the process, business requirements can be defined in more detail, thus helping to avoid scope "creep", where later, incremental changes to the system delay the delivery of the core product.

Data Configuration: Many ETRM solutions come with pre-packaged components that need to be heavily configured by the vendor to fit the specific needs of the client. The vendor typically leads this configuration effort to ensure the base package components are configured properly. This phase will include gathering and loading initial master data, such as contract details, book structure, trading and delivery locations, price reference data, counterparty and broker data, trading and credit limits, etc. The configuration effort also includes establishing user groups, the security schema and the workflow-management process. Wherever possible, requirements should be met through the standard product configuration, or where there are gaps, through external solutions. Extensive customization of the product, particularly through tailored software coding, should be avoided. The complexity of future upgrades increases significantly if a customer is running on a branched or non-standard code set.

Reporting: Many organizations incorrectly assume that they can leverage the "canned" suite of reports provided as part of the vendor package. The reality is that these base-product components usually require additional customization and do not typically meet clients' needs. It is important to define detailed requirements and specifications at project inception and to budget adequate development time. In our experience, the potential set of reports that a business may choose to define can be large, and this forms a significant proportion of an implementation project's configuration and testing effort. To avoid putting the overall implementation at risk, a pragmatic approach should be adopted to defining a core set of business critical reports as part of the first release. Buyers also should consider the ease with which additional reports can be created later.

Data Migration: Many implementations are a replacement of one ETRM system with another. A key component that often receives insufficient attention is the migration of data from the original system to the new database. This requires the mapping of reference data, and we generally advocate the creation of automated ETL (Extract, Transfer and Load) routines to support this process. This generally needs to be rehearsed a number of times with frequent and significant reconciliations to validate the success of the migration. Live execution of these routines then forms a key part of the cutover process. In addition, the business need to store transaction data history (e.g. for prior period reporting or for audit purposes) needs to be balanced against the potential degradation of performance if too large a data volume is retained.

Testing: Once the ETRM system configuration has been completed, the product is ready for testing. As with any new application development or product implementation, testing is an integral part of the project. Throughout each phase of testing, any discrepancies or problems should be documented and analyzed by the testing team, in conjunction with the product vendor. Problems and issues should be logged, prioritized and communicated to the product vendor in a timely and detailed manner. Procedures for problem resolution should be clearly documented in the vendor contract.

Parallel Testing

Because transitioning to a new trading system poses significant risk, we advocate a parallel-run period as part of the cutover. This requires both the new and legacy systems to run in parallel (e.g. double trade entry and approval) and can therefore be a challenging component of any ETRM implementation because it presents operational risk and requires the business users to support both systems. The objective is to operate these systems in a production-like environment to compare and reconcile data inputs, processing, and outputs between the applications. The effort also will provide an environment for users to learn and become comfortable with new system functionality prior to final deployment. Needless to say, this effort will be time intensive for both the project team and user groups.

Structure has found it helpful to implement a parallel test that mirrors all operations throughout a monthly trading cycle. Typically, it makes sense to start with the critical daily processes during the initial weeks (trade entry, price updates, confirmations, risk management, daily reporting, credit, contract administration, scheduling). Monthly processes can be tested during the later weeks (settlements, actualization, invoicing, cash application, accruals, AR/AP aging, etc).

It is also important to prepare automated daily reconciliation reports to compare trade and price entry between systems to ensure that the key inputs into both systems match. In addition, a separate set of reports should be developed that compares key system outputs such as positions, trade/market value, mark-to-market at the trade level. Having these tools readily available on a daily basis makes this difficult process much more manageable.

User Acceptance Testing

The acceptance of the system signals the client's approval of the software from the product vendor. Business users should be responsible for accepting the application, and submitting a recommendation of approval to an overall Project Steering Committee. Once official product acceptance has been received, the system should be ready for deployment. User acceptance testing also provides an opportunity for users to become more acquainted with how the new system will support their business processes. In essence, it becomes part of the training component of the implementation.

Performance Testing

The system's performance is key to a successful implementation. It should be a top priority from the demonstration and selection process onward. Demonstration scenarios should take performance into account, because a system that demos well with a small subset of simple trades may get bogged down with a large portfolio of complex instruments.

Where possible, concrete performance benchmarks should be established and included in the vendor contract. This gives the buyer leverage with the vendor should promised performance not live up to expectations.

Training and Rollout

All users should be trained based on the modules of the system that map directly to their role. Training should cover both application and business-process training. At a high level, the following types of training should be provided:

- **System Administration Training** – Training for the key technical owner of the application. This user typically has full and unrestricted access to all functionality in the application, and should be trained accordingly.
- **Super User Training** – Training for the key business owner of the application. This user is typically responsible for the configuration and maintenance of the system in production mode.
- **Role-based User Training** – Training for each user role defined in the system.
- **Technical Training** – Training for IT technical resources to support the application without assistance from the vendor (which usually incurs additional costs).

Upon acceptance and the completion of training, the system should be deployed to all users. It is important that support staff from the vendor be available for several weeks to address issues and questions as business users get acclimated to the new product and its processes on a daily basis.

Lessons Learned

Through our experience performing vendor-package implementations, we have learned several practical and valuable lessons.

- Aligning business processes with the underlying workflows embedded in the application design requires more planning, although the pay off is significant. Structure has found that companies who have modified business processes to fit vendor functionality have:

  (a) required little or no base code changes;

  (b) attained significant amounts of functionality from vendor applications; and

  (c) avoided post-implementation remediation initiatives.

  Structure has found that it is critical for the buyer to allow the vendor to explain the "as-designed" workflows and adopt these to the fullest extent possible. Fortunately, the top ETRM vendors generally follow basic processes that are well defined, understood, and will fit most business requirements. Nonetheless, it is imperative to communicate and agree to any business process changes the product may introduce as early as possible.

- Active user participation and management commitment is critical throughout the project. The value of this should not be underestimated in the early stages of the project when it is easier to influence change. Many successful projects appoint an executive sponsor and Project Steering Committee to champion the effort and attain management and user commitment. In addition, the project sponsor and steering committee should provide executive guidance and project direction.

- These types of projects require experienced and dedicated implementation resources that have "done this before" to mitigate project delays, budget overruns and scope creep. In addition, it is crucial to ensure management supports and communicates resource allocation by establishing a project charter and an organization chart that clearly sets out individuals and their responsibilities. Furthermore, internal project resources need to be able to balance their ongoing workload with the additional project responsibilities.

- Structure believes that experienced project managers can bridge the functional and communication gap between IT and business stakeholders and between the client and the vendor. In addition, it is important to supplement the project team with resources who have product, business and implementation expertise.

- When implementing a new system, delivery pressure can result in a system delivered at an unacceptable level of quality and functionality. It is important to conduct thorough due diligence with the vendor during procurement and contracting. Consider including payment/penalty milestones in vendor contracts. Develop realistic budget estimates, resource allocations and project timelines. For complex implementations, consider a phased implementation approach that allows urgent and critical functionality to be delivered as part of an initial release.

- Knowledge transfer from the project implementation team to the operational team should not be overlooked. Structure recommends staffing the initial project team with the operational personnel who will be maintaining the system to ensure a smooth transition and mitigate any go-live risks.

- Reporting is typically more complex and difficult to develop than initially anticipated. It is important to understand that in some products, data is easily assessable through a relational database structure, while others require translating data from a normalized into a de-normalized format via a reporting database tool. It is important to determine the challenges so that staff with the requisite experience are assigned to the project.

- Much like reporting, it is important to note that some products use proprietary development languages for scripting, reporting and customization. This often makes the product more difficult to implement and maintain over the long term because those specialized skills can be difficult to find.

While ETRM system implementations are a difficult undertaking, they are surmountable with the appropriate level of resources, commitment, knowledge and management. At Structure, our objective is to provide clients with the skills and knowledge to reduce delivery risk, increase efficiency and ensure success.

Focus Topic I

Understanding the ETRM Vendor Business Model

Mr. Patrick Reames.

UtiliPoint International, Inc.

ETRM systems are an expensive proposition for any company. Even
for the smallest organizations, the cost to acquire, implement, and
maintain these systems represent a significant capital outlay.
According to UtiliPoint data, the smallest shops can expect to pay over
a half a million dollars to the vendor of the system during the life of
that system – the largest companies can expect to pay up to 10 million
dollars or more (not including costs associated with ancillary systems
and integration). Given this investment, and the reliance your business
has on the system, it's important to understand not only the capabilities
of the system, but also of the vendor who built and maintains that

system. As a client, you will be working closely with that vendor over the life of the system, relying on them for expertise, training, support and maintenance. As your business grows, changes, and evolves, your vendor will need to ensure that your system maintains pace. Choosing the capable system from a vendor that cannot maintain that pace will lead to disaster. Many companies have found themselves stranded on a system, without support, because their vendor of choice disappeared into the ether of bad business decision making.

As stated in previous sections of this book, there are many capable ETRM systems on the market. However, the history of the ETRM space shows that producing a capable product is not enough – the vendor must also navigate the complexities of selling that software system to a market of limited size. Many customers in the past have found themselves stranded on an unsupported product when their chosen vendor had either closed its doors or had been acquired by another when they were unable to sustain themselves.

Complex Systems/Small Market

2007 was a record year for most software vendors. While a significant portion of the sales were replacements of existing systems, new market entrants, particularly in the form of banks and hedge funds drove, helped drive market growth. Additionally, power market restructuring, taking place in California and Texas drove many utilities to seek new solutions to better manage their business in those markets.

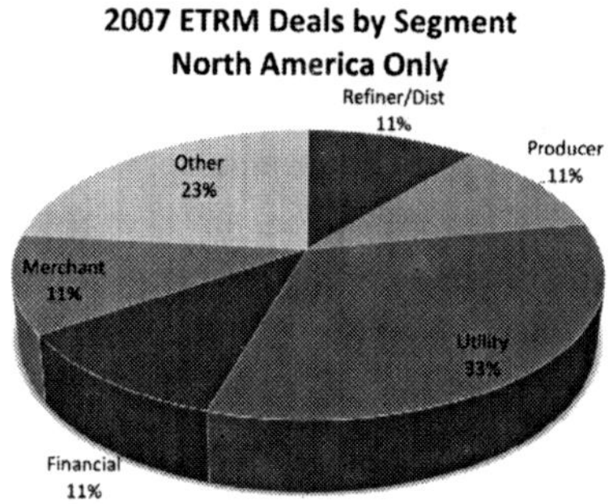

While record sales may indicate an active market, additional research by UtiliPoint indicates that the commercially available systems still fall short in terms of their being able to answer the entirety of the needs of the market place. A recent study by

Figure 1: 2007 ETRM Deals by Market Segment

2007 ETRM Deals by Segment
North America Only

UtiliPoint, in which we polled users of commercially supported ETRM solutions, indicated that for most multi-commodity trading organizations, even after implementation of the latest generation of ETRM systems, spreadsheets were still utilized to some degree in the information chain. While not reflecting broad failure on the part of the systems vendors, the result does indicate that some deficiencies exist.

Additional studies conducted by UtiliPoint point to some level of dissatisfaction with vendor supported systems, although those systems do have a higher level of satisfaction than the alternatives, such as custom developed systems or spreadsheets. In the 2005 Natural Gas Benchmarking Study[3], about 25% of users of vendor systems reported they felt the systems were not fully effective in managing their business (Figure 2).

Figure 2: Effectiveness by Type of Solution

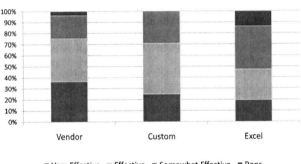

■ Very Effective   ▨ Effective   ■ Somewhat Effective   ■ Poor

So, despite the sales success of the vendors in today's market, indications are that they are failing to meet the all the needs of the market. This failure can be attributed to several factors. The most widely accepted measure of success for any software company is new license sales. As these companies seek out new clients, there has been a historical willingness to commit to development of new features or functionality to attract new clients, even if that committed feature or function is not a requirement of their broader client base. This is not to say that most are willing to do pure customization of their core code, but they will include additional features for a relatively minor segment of the market if they feel that segment will provide some new sales. This type of development activity can come at the expense of changes and/or upgrades that are requested by the majority of the vendors' clients. Additional development pressures come from changes needed to maintain clients' compliance with regulatory mandates, such as development of functionality that was required in order to ensure compliance with Sarbanes Oxley legislation.

In virtually every case, new functionality is an expansion of code. Feature and functions are added, but rarely are elements removed from the code. The experience of the industry has been that if you provide a feature to a client, they will find some use for it, even if it's not its original intended purpose. Removing any of these features will create client issues and endanger the support and maintenance revenue stream for the vendor. It is this prospect of client losses that has prevented ETRM vendors from being able to leverage the latest technologies and bring true innovation to the wholesale energy trading market.

Difficulty in Driving Innovation in the ETRM Market

Vendors of ETRM systems are faced with a difficult balancing act. Technology advances create expectations in the market that software products should leverage the best available technologies. However, given the breadth and depth of functionality of ETRM systems, driving technology innovation can be extremely difficult, time consuming, and expensive.

As previously noted, vendors are constantly forced to allocate limited resource to meet the demands of various stake holders. Stockholders expectations, even in privately held corporations, are that any enterprise should demonstrate growth. For traditional software companies, of which most ETRM vendors can be considered, growth is best demonstrated by year over year increases in license revenue. However, an additional component of an ETRM vendor's revenue stream is support and maintenance payments derived from their base of licensed users. Most vendors in this market will charge an annual support and maintenance fee equivalent to 18 to 20% of the list license fee. As their client base grows, this revenue becomes a very significant part of their overall revenue structure. A loss of any client can represent a significant impact to the company's bottom line, particularly in a market place of limited size such as this one (UtiliPoint estimates that the revenue associated with license sales of ETRM systems was approximately $115 million in 2007).

As the client base grows, so do the demands placed upon the vendors support staff and development organization. Code issues and functional deficiencies become more obvious and more urgent with an increase in user count as more eyes are exploring the depths of the systems. Additionally, many clients will not stay current with the vendor release cycle, despite contractual obligations to do so. Unfortunately, for many vendors, past releases were of poor quality, leading clients to decline to take new release and demand that they be supported on their installed version. In doing so, they are forcing vendors to keep open code streams that should have been closed and brought forward to the latest version releases. There have been very recent instances of vendors supporting more than 6 versions of the same product, running on two different databases, creating more than a dozen versions of a single product that must be managed. In these types of instances, the costs of providing level two support can be enormous and draw down the ability of the vendor to dedicate development resources to bring innovation to the product.

However, even if a vendor had no constraints on development resources, re-architecting an ETRM system to take true advantage of technology improvements can be a daunting task. Again, due to 1) the complexity of the applications and the scope of the business processes they represent and 2) the evolutionary development that has occurred for most of these products, the underlying data structures are not fully optimized in order to advantage of the new technologies. While some vendors have been able to move parts of their systems forward to a .net or java environment, they have been limited to making less than wholesale changes to the structure of the database. If they were to do so, they would lose the ability to programmatically move their clients forward from version to version, requiring that those clients essentially re-implement the new product. Given the costs in term of dollars and time of a full blown implementation effort, any client faced with such a prospect would most likely start to review their options to 1) commit to the costly implementation effort, 2) refuse to move and demand support on the current version, or 3) review the offering available from other vendors. As a software vendor, unless you can create an extremely compelling value proposition, you're going to have extreme difficultly convincing the client that the benefit of a technology change will be worth the effort, particularly as the first release under that new architecture would probably be at best equivalent to the old version in terms of functionality.

Given these harsh realities, and as mentioned previously, ETRM software vendors are generally consigned to making step changes, utilizing limited development resources to make incremental improvements in technology while working to ensure they retain their client base by not creating product upgrade cycles are too costly for the clients to manage.

Despite the difficulties faced by many ETRM vendors, many of the systems available today are actually quite effective and do provide significant functionality improvements over previous product generations. Those vendors that have proven successful over the long term have been able to overcome, to some extent, the inherent issues faced in servicing energy trading.

In some cases the vendors where able to enter the market with a product from the financial services markets, making their first offering somewhat innovative from the outset, not having been tied to the "traditional" physical natural gas model that so many of the incumbent vendors were struggling with, a model that while effective for that particular market segment, constrained the developers and forced them into making compromises as they tried to expand their products to meet the needs of the broader market. In fact two of the top five "full spectrum" ETRM vendors (those that provide multi-commodity, physical/financial systems capable of managing transactions from contract initiation through logistics through invoicing) entered the energy trading markets after having success in the financial markets.

Working with Your Vendor of Choice

While most clients of ETRM software providers would like to believe they are operating in partnership with their chosen vendor, the reality is, many times, different. Larger customers will almost always command the most attention from vendors as they can apply the most commercial leverage (they are, after all, the vendors' largest source of support and maintenance revenue). However, vendors will also value those relationships for more than revenue, as the largest trading groups can provide them with valuable insight into future design and development requirements for the market as a whole, as these groups tend to be closer to the "leading edge" of the market than are smaller shops. There have been cases in the past of a product vendor deferring development of functionality desired by the majority of their client base in order to meet the short term needs of one or two of their largest clients. In these cases, the needs of the few outweighed the needs of the many. Certainly, the ETRM software market is not unique in this regard. In any commercial endeavor, a product provider will always seek to first satisfy the market segment that provides the greatest return.

Unfortunately, for smaller customers, this can be a harsh reality. It's all too easy for a small customer's needs to get set aside when global trading shops start making demands with loud voices and heavy hands. So, what is a smaller shop to do? They still require the functionality provided by these systems, and as their businesses grow and evolve, they need those systems to keep up. They cannot afford to have required enhancements to their mission critical applications held hostage to the demands of others.

For a smaller company, it's important to "right size" your purchase decision. Many times companies will default to the market leader, the vendor that is selling the most systems and servicing the top tier of the energy trading market place. On the surface it's the safe decision, the least risky. If the big trading houses like the vendor, it's easy to defend your purchase decision. The problem is that vendor is probably producing the most sophisticated application, one that services global market players. Is that what you are? It's important to ask yourself, "do you need the latest and greatest risk analytics; commodity coverage that can manage every conceivable product from apples to zebra skins, and a technology stack utilizing middleware and the latest .Net capabilities?" If not, you should set aside your natural inclination to follow the leader and explore the options provided by many of the smaller solutions vendors in the market. These smaller vendors, many of which cover only gas and/or power or other single commodities, specialize in the mid and lower tiers of the market. They produce very workable solutions that may include solid risk management tools, scheduling/logistics, and strong accounting functionality. Additionally, these smaller vendors will generally be priced well below the industry leader.

Should you, as a smaller shop, choose to go with one of the leaders, be sure to check not only the references provided by the vendor, but also use your own network of contacts to find others that are using their systems. Ask about their support history – has the vendor followed through on their promises, delivering improved functionality to all their clients on time, or has delivery of enhancements been delayed for an extended amount of time due some less than acceptable reason? Learn about their client base. Does their list of customers include others like you? Does the company understand the issues of your market, not focus solely on the needs of the upper tier?

Once you've identified your vendor and product of choice, be certain that any needed changes to the product are fully documented and included in the license agreements. Contractual obligations will always carry more weight than a handshake and heartfelt promise.

Lastly, many ETRM software vendors have active user groups, either organized and supported directly by the company or independent of, but actively cooperating with the vendor. In some cases, the vendor will have an agreement in place with their user group to set aside some number of development hours that will be dedicated annually to developing functionally and enhancements brought forth from the group. If it's a contractual obligation between the vendor and the user group, all the better.

ETRM SOLUTIONS AND "THE DISCIPLINE OF MARKET LEADERS"

M. Patrick Reames,

UtiliPoint International, Inc.

A senior executive at an ETRM software vendor mentioned to me that his management team was discussing strategy and had focused the discussion on the theories expounded in the book "The Discipline of Market Leaders"[3] authored by Michael Treacy & Fred Wiersema, first published in 1995. For those unfamiliar with the book (and I'll have to partially include myself in that category, having heard the theory but not really being familiar with the source), the authors advanced the notion that truly successful organizations embrace a singular value

---

[3] Treacy, Micheal, Fred Wiersema. The Discipline of Market Leaders. New York: Basic Books, 1995.

proposition and align their organizations around that value proposition. In Treacy and Wiersema's book, they identified three distinct value propositions that companies can follow to achieve a market leadership position:

1. Operationally Efficient - In an operationally efficient company, it's all about the delivery of products and services in the most (as the name implies) efficient and effective manner. These companies are highly process oriented and highly productive. They generally get their products out the door quickly and cheaply. Their customers get reliable products and services; and the company is pretty easy to do business with. You're not getting a leading edge product, but you can be sure that what you're getting will generally meet your expectations and at a price that is lower than the competition. Examples of companies that follow this model are Wal-Mart, McDonalds and Dell.

2. Product Leader – In a company embracing product leadership, the focus is on identifying, understanding and responding to market needs, both current and future, and in the process providing the best, most advanced and innovative products. These companies are creative, innovative risk takers. In doing business with these companies, you're getting the best product in the category. However, you're going to be paying a premium for that leading edge product. Example companies for this category include Apple, Sony and 3M.

3. Customer Intimate – Customer intimate organizations strive to understand the customer intimately and provide the best total solution. In the process, they strive to gain customer loyalty and develop long-term relationships. These companies are friendly, responsive and adaptable to customer demands. As a customer you're not only getting a customized, personalized product, you're also getting a trusted advisor and partner. However, when you're doing business with these companies, you're paying top dollar.

Companies that fit this model include Nordstrom and Ritz Carlton.

In the authors' view, in order for any company to achieve the status of "market leader", no matter the industry or market they serve, they must embrace one of these value propositions, both internally and externally, and always focus their efforts to achieve the goals that they have elaborated in the adoption of the proposition. Additionally, no company can embrace all three, they must focus on one and do the best they can with the other two, but never to the determent of their chosen value proposition. The theory implies that trying to be all things to everybody will lead to the inevitable state of being nothing for anyone.

The theory is still very popular and widely used today, and it's easy to see why. Focus and discipline are universally accepted as qualities that are necessary for anyone or any company to succeed, and applying those traits around a central value proposition would seem to almost guarantee success (if you truly have a product and a market that wants it).

Applying the "Discipline" theory to ETRM Products and Markets

However, applying the "Discipline" theory to ETRM solutions vendors can be problematic. The market for these products is extremely small when compared to almost all consumer products, and further, you can divide this small market up into even smaller discreet segments, grouped by commodity, geography, or business model.

Consider this group of fictional companies:

- A small west Texas gas producer sells equity production and schedules gas on a handful of pipelines.
- A Washington state merchant power producer sells power from multiple units into two ISO's, requiring real-time scheduling.

- A Wall Street energy trading company takes positions in virtually every energy commodity across the country. They trade both physically and financially.
- A large Chicago based airline tracks JetA fuel purchases at 3 regional hubs in the US and two international hubs. They hedge these purchases whenever its makes sense.
- A global energy company is involved in the production of almost all hydrocarbon products world-wide and markets their products on five continents.

The small gas producer and the merchant generator would probably want to do business with vendors that have embraced the operationally efficient model, a vendor that can provide a low cost product that while not leading edge, still meets their somewhat "generic" needs. These companies probably wouldn't be interested in a "total ownership" experience given that what they do, while not easy, is pretty straightforward. They aren't really looking for a solution partnership, just a product.

The Wall Street firm however, is going to be depending on their ETRM solution to help make them money. They will want a product that can keep up with their needs. They view themselves as a trading shop, not an IT shop, and therefore rely on their vendor to be more than just a software supplier; they want the vendor to be their partner, ensuring that they have the vendor's ear and access to their talent to ensure their systems never hold them back. Clearly, this is a company that would place high value on a Customer Intimate experience.

The airline will be looking to their vendor to provide them with a product that can capture the single commodity (JetA fuel) both physically and financially, but in multiple currencies and possibly in multiple units of measure. Their IT staff is probably not going to have significant experience in these types of systems, so they will most likely be looking to the vendor to supply ongoing support and services, similar to that of the Wall Street firm, but in a less intensive mode.

The global energy producer may have a very large global IT organization. In their business they need a large support staff, not only to service the marketing organization, but also the exploration, production, and refining groups. They have a sophisticated marketing operation and because of their geographic reach, they trade products in all the major market regions around the globe. This is a company looking for a leading edge product, one that they can deploy to address their marketing needs now and that will keep up with their growth. Given the size and experience of their IT staff, they're self-sufficient and aren't looking to the vendor to be a partner. They want to do business with a product leader.

Most of the major ETRM software vendors will view each of those companies as a potential customer for their products. Clearly, the needs of the west Texas gas producer have very small overlap with the needs of the Wall Street firm or the global producer; and the needs of an airline or a merchant generator have even less. Yet in these days of multi-commodity, physical/financial ETRM products, a single vendor will visit all five and demonstrate how the capabilities of their product(s) might meet the needs of these companies.

The Vendor Perspective

So, how does a single vendor address the needs of this heterogeneous market and what are the implications for that vendor when trying to establish their value proposition?

In some cases, the vendors in the ETRM market still develop their products around a monolithic code base. They may disable some features and/or functions depending on the client needs; but, it's still the same code serving the small west Texas producer and the Wall Street trader. It costs the same to produce for both customers, but it is sold at different prices. Given that the vendor's investment in the product was made to address the needs of the top end of the market (the global multi-commodity, physical/financial trader), that vendor will have a very difficult time elaborating a value proposition that makes sense for the small producer market. The market segments are clearly different and have different business drivers. It is impossible for a single product to be stretched over a fractionated market and meet the expectations of the majority of the players therein. So, this vendor would need to focus on that high end market, define their value proposition in terms of that piece of the market, and just do the best they can for the rest, risking a significant amount of market share in the process.

Given the difficulties in developing a market wide value proposition for their product and their company, and if one assumes that the "Discipline" theory is valid, the vendor of the monolithic product is probably not going to become the market leader in the broader ETRM space. They could lead a niche market, but for the majority of the market, they will find themselves in the position of trying to be everything to everybody, with the attendant result.

However, if the vendor can supply a product set built around a modular, service oriented architecture, and deployed with a common integration infrastructure, that vendor can start to view the market as the heterogeneous environment that it is, and develop specific strategies and products to address the different segments. Each combination of market segment and product module can potentially be oriented as a separate entity, all rolling up to the vendor parent. The selection of the value proposition for these separate entities could then be undertaken using the processes outlined in Treacy and Wiersema's book; based upon standardized metrics, including the cost to service, and the value expectations of, the various market segments.

The Buyer Side

So, what does this mean for the buyers of ETRM systems? It means that you must understand and clearly express your expectations to the vendor, and ensure that vendor's value proposition (either explicit or implied) is aligned to meet those expectations. If your's is one of the smaller operations, trading only gas or only power, and you don't have aspirations of triple digit year-over-year growth, the answer may be that you want to do business with an operationally efficient vendor that can give you a decent product at a lower price. If you don't require leading edge functionality, you'll probably find that it's good enough.

However, if you're working for a growing international trading company that takes both physical and financial positions in gas, power, coal, crude, and NGL's; the low cost provider solution is going to be wholly inadequate. The scale and scope of your business dictate that you need the latest functionality. It may even mean that your company's business is unique enough that you need a somewhat customized solution. You're going to be seeking out a product and a vendor that can maintain your pace. Given your circumstances, your vendor will either need to be the superior technology company or the full service, customer intimate organization. But, you should be prepared to pay the cost associated with the product and service level you expect to receive. Trying to buy and implement a sophisticated ETRM solution on the cheap is a receipt for disaster.

You can't expect to shop at Nordstrom and pay Wal-Mart prices.

FOCUS TOPIC III

MANAGING HISTORICAL TRANSACTIONAL DATA

Mr. Patrick Reames,

UtiliPoint International, Inc.

When implementing a new ETRM system, a critical decision point is
what to do with historical transactions – those deals that are complete
and no longer in effect. Obviously a company cannot just "throw them
away" by decommissioning the old system and deleting the old
database. For transactions less than a year or two old, prior period
adjustments remain a real possibility. Companies need to have access
to these transactions in order to ensure that the accounting for prior
period adjustments is correct and recorded appropriately. Additionally,
audit requirements will necessitate that these transaction records are
accessible for several years. So, since it's not just a matter of turning
off the old system on the day that the new system goes live, what do

you do? There are several options available. The first is to programmatically move the old transactions to the new system.

Programmatic Data Transfers

In a perfect world, you could just run a software program that would scrape out the database from the old system and load the appropriate information into the new. Unfortunately, unless the new system is an update of the old, or the new system was built off the architecture of the old, the ability to transfer these types of transactional data is limited, and in some cases, practically impossible.

To clarify, let's define transactional data. Transitional data would include deals, schedule or paths, actualized volumes and the associated accounting entries. It would not include more static types of information such as pipelines, grids, meters, pools, or enabling agreements such as service contracts or bilateral marketing contracts – otherwise known as enabling agreements. When we talk about transactional data we are talking about the unique combination of an enabling agreement, a specific term (hours, days, months, years, etc), a commodity volume, a point (e.g. combination of pipe and meter), and a price. We would also include the logistical components of managing that transaction or deal. This would include any transactions associated to it including pooling, pathing, or scheduling. It is this unique combination of deal elements and logistical activity that creates a unique set of records for every ETRM system.

Some systems will dictate that each point associated with a deal must be treated as a new deal record, meaning that if you buy a single volume or package of gas or power from a counterparty, but they want you to pick it up at two different locations, some systems will require that the transaction be represented by two "deals", that is two transactions with unique deal numbers. Other systems will allow you to have multiple points under the "deal", with both discreet volumes represented by a single deal number.

Moving further down the value chain, any deal must be scheduled or pathed in order to associate it with an offsetting transaction – think source and sink, or buy and sell. Even if the screens used to create these associations are somewhat similar between two systems from different vendors, the underlying representations of the data in the databases might be wildly dissimilar. Every vendor has adopted a database schema and data structures that operate most effectively and efficiently for their particular system and chosen technology stack. There are no standard database schema or data structures yet in commercially available ETRM systems.

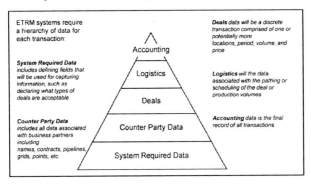

Should you wish to programmatically move the transactional data from System A (supplied Vendor X) to System B (supplied by Vendor Y), you would need to develop (after a long period of analysis) scripts that would extract the data from the legacy database, perform appropriate data transformations, and load that data into the new system in a manner that it would accept, taking into consideration the unique requirements of that system's data validation rules – meaning the component fields of the transactions have to match data elements that have, by necessity, been preloaded in the new system. This means that for any particular counterparty with which you've done a deal, you will need to have preloaded all information about that counterparty, including company name, traders' names, addresses, phone numbers, etc. You will also need to have created the enabling agreement for that counterparty, meaning contract type, terms and conditions, and all other associated information.

Bottom line, the data will need to be built up layer-by-layer prior to any transactional data being loaded; meaning that every data field required by the new system will need to be populated prior to capturing a transaction. Conceivably, one could attempt to circumvent the data validation rules of the new system, however, if you are successful at doing so, you will most likely end up corrupting the database, rendering it useless and invalidating your support agreement.

There are other considerations to take into account. The legacy database will need to be analyzed to identify all the fields that comprise a "deal". It is not a simple matter of finding a record called "deal" and pulling that out. A deal record will most likely be dispersed throughout the database, linked by multiple key fields. Identifying the right keys and data fields will require someone with intimate knowledge of the application and database. In many cases, the only person with that level of knowledge will be a resource of the company that designed and built the product. Calling the vendor of the system that you are replacing and asking for their assistance in making you more successful on their competitor's system will probably get you a very icy reception.

In light of the complexities of attempting to programmatically transfer historical transaction data, such an undertaking is probably going to be very expensive and risk laden. There will be numerous technical and business resources required to accomplish the task, and it will most likely be a process of trial and error before success can be declared. Additionally, as the process of developing workable software scripts will involve iterative trial and error, it will create difficulties in developing a solid project plan, requiring significant contingencies to be built into that plan. It's these types of complex and risky sub-projects within the overall implementation effort that can lead to stalled and/or ultimately failed projects.

An Alternative

If it is deemed necessary, for whatever reason, to have historical transactional data in the newly implemented system, a possible alternative to the development of a programmatic solution would be to input the transactions manually. This would be a workable solution only for companies that have a limited number of transactions, no more than a few hundred, as the transactions not only have to be input, but they must also be pathed or scheduled and rolled into the accounting function in order to be of any real value. Additionally, it's not a case of just getting it done in as timely a manner as possible, but the effort must be audited to ensure that the transactions were captured and managed accurately. Clearly, for all but the smallest of businesses, manually inputting the historical transaction data (also know as front-end loading) is simply not a viable alternative given the time and effort required to capture vast amounts of information.

The Best Choice?

In light of the complexity, risks and costs associated with trying to programmatically load historical transactions; and the effort required to "front end load" these transactions, a third alternative offers probably the best path forward for most companies – *leave the historical transactions where they are.* Don't try to recreate history in your new system, rather keep the old system in minimal use, accessing it only for reporting and accounting purposes.

Most commercial software licenses are perpetual – meaning that you can continue to use the software indefinitely at no cost. Once you terminate your agreements with the system vendor, you won't have support and maintenance, however, if all you are using the system for is to access and possibly adjust old transactions, it is very unlikely that any issues would arise that would require the vendor involvement (and even if you ultimately did have any issues, you could request time and material support). Additionally, by limiting the access to the old system to a few select "need to know" users, you will help to ensure the integrity of the old data as well as minimize the load on the system, and the chance that someone could possibly "screw something up".

Obviously, having your business data in multiple systems is not ideal. However, given the alternatives, it will likely make the most sense from a cost/benefit standpoint. However, keep these "rules" in mind:

1. Limit the number of users that have access to the old system to those that absolutely need it, i.e. accounting/audit personnel and a few designated trading staff.

2. If possible, create a "data mart" of the deals by downloading them to Excel. This will allow traders

to refer back to their past transactions for analysis. Many of the commercially available systems have the ability to download a "deals report" to Excel.

3. Move the historical database and application to its own dedicated server and keep the technology on that server static if possible. Don't attempt to keep it up with the latest technology, just the most stable. This will reduce the possibility of encountering or creating "bugs" with the old system.

BE AWARE OF THE COSTS OF THE TWENTY PERCENT

Mr. Patrick Reames,

UtiliPoint International, Inc.

I recently had a conversation with an unnamed senior manager at an unnamed major producer/marketer (yes, I am purposefully being coy in order to protect the innocent here). He was describing, in a manner I found curiously casual, the fact that he had recently discovered that his company was being overcharged (and had been for several months) by a major pipeline to the tune of more than $300,000 per month. As the conversation progressed, I asked how it was possible that such an issue was not caught earlier, because, from my perspective, $300,000 is a lot of money. It turns out that the company was lucky it was caught at all. It was only discovered when senior management had asked for an economic evaluation of a particular field that was flowing into that pipeline. The person who was helping pull together the data happened to notice that the costs allocated back to the properties didn't quite look right and did a little research and ultimately discovered the problem, meaning if senior management hadn't asked for the unrelated ad-hoc report, the problem may have gone unnoticed.

I asked about the process for invoice approval and how the invoice was ultimately approved for payment even though it was wrong. Didn't they have payable statements from their ETRM system that provided detail of each transportation agreement, the volumes that flowed under that agreement, and ultimately the costs for the period? He said that sure, in most cases they do. Most cases? "Well, some agreements are just too complex to capture in the system." This was one of those agreements. The discount structure was "too complex" to efficiently capture and would have created pathing and scheduling issues; so, they relied on their T&E representative to send an email to the accountant responsible for that pipe, notifying them that gas they were moving to an alternate point under that particular agreement was supposed to be discounted. Unfortunately, the T&E representative got busy and forgot. When the invoice came in from the pipeline, they were erroneously charged the full rate for all delivery points under the agreement, and since it matched what was in the company's ETRM system, it was approved for payment.

The 80/20 Rule

For anyone who has been involved in more than a single ETRM implementation, this situation won't be particularly surprising. It all goes back to the 80/20 rule of ETRM, which has evolved to state that being able to manage 80% of your business in the system was pretty much as good as it gets; the 20% is that piece of your business that is so unique or so difficult to model that it just isn't worth the time and expense of developing functionality to capture it. These would be the "workarounds", those things that would be addressed more or less by process and spreadsheets, or more likely, more by spreadsheet and less by process. Users accept this as a given, acknowledging that "it is what it is".

The problem is, in this environment of consistently high prices and sometimes startling volatility, the exposure of the "20%" is greater than ever. Even in a world dominated by Sarbanes Oxley process maps, these workaround processes and spreadsheets find a way to break down. Complex spreadsheets having a way of getting corrupted even by experienced users, where a small change to a single formula ripples unnoticed throughout other formulas and creates answers, that although directionally correct, are just enough wrong to cost a company thousands or tens of thousands of dollars on a monthly basis. A process designed to ensure the relevant people are kept up-to-date and that loops monthly can get derailed by an unnoticed or unsent email.

> *The ETRM 80/20 rule should not be confused with Pereto's Principle which has been stated many ways, but ultimately means that 80% of the effect comes from 20% of the effort.*

Virtually all energy marketing/trading companies have some form of these workarounds and have learned to accept them as business as usual. However, as these workarounds were devised when the ETRM system was installed and implemented, and as UtiliPoint data indicates that the *average* life of an installed ETRM system for gas is about 6.5 years, simple math indicates that the exposure is much greater now with gas prices trading consistently north of $6, as opposed to the $2-$3 range when the system was likely first deployed. Even with Sarbanes Oxley forcing companies to formally document many of the processes; it doesn't change the fact that these workarounds are isolated from the more systematic business flow that is captured in the transaction management system; meaning that there is a greater likelihood of there being multiple points of failure. These failures are most likely not going to be catastrophic, as a complete failure is probably going to be quickly noticed. No, they will tend to be more erosive, as in when someone forgets to update a price and/or a formula in a spreadsheet, or forgets to send the email to the accountant indicating that a portion of gas deal got scheduled to an alternate delivery point on a particular day and that the discounted transportation cost is not reflected in the system because the rate structure was too difficult or time consuming to model.

So, what's the point? Even the best ETRM systems are prone to user error aren't they? Yes, they are, but with a central repository of information, errors are more easily recognized and corrected. Data and events are chained together, meaning that multiple eyes are seeing and implicitly reviewing the information as it passes through the system. Pricing and volumetric information can be looked at on a trended basis, highlighting any anomalous data points. The more visibility, the more likely errors will be caught and corrected.

Reduce the 20% and Your Operational Exposure

The latest generation ETRM systems provide more flexibility in capturing those unique deals and transactions that once required workarounds. Even for those deals that are the result of creative "price structuring", or for negotiated transportation agreements that contain volumetric or rate optionality, there is likely a solution available in the market that will help reduce the number of workarounds in your organization. However, even the most sophisticated system will probably not be able to explicitly model every transaction for every user. For those instances, many of the vendors have created programmatic interfaces to Excel, allowing users to tie their workaround spreadsheet directly to the system, helping to reduce the chances of keying errors, and also bringing the spreadsheets closer to the core processes, and in turn, helping to improve their visibility to the rest of the enterprise.

Even if your system is relatively new, having been implemented in the last two or three years, given the potential cost of errors, it is worthwhile to be constantly reviewing your workarounds, both in terms of finding ways to incorporate them into the latest version release of your system, and in terms of ensuring that potential profits are not eroded by breakdowns in data or process.

Take another look at determining whether it's worthwhile to develop a programmatic solution to the workaround. Escalating commodity prices will in many cases shift the economic decision point. Spending tens of thousands of dollars to save hundreds of thousands is pretty much a no-brainer. However, do not ignore the ongoing costs of a partially customized solution. Future support costs and potential impacts on upgrading product versions must be part of the equation. Development of custom code can be a costly affair when that code must be rewritten every time you deploy a new version of the application for which it was developed. A sound development methodology for these types of custom solutions would ensure that the new code is as non-invasive to the core application as possible.

Alternatively, work with your ETRM vendor to determine if they can incorporate your required functionality into their system. What may have been unique to your business two years ago, may in fact be a more widely adopted business process now and is something that many of your peer companies need to address with programmatic solution.

Bottom line, the 20% is where most of the errors are likely to occur and propagate. By reducing that number, you can reduce the likely that your profits are being eroded.

This Focus Topic is based upon the UtiliPoint International IssueAlert "The Erosive Costs of the Twenty Percent" by Patrick Reames, published Oct. 20, 2006.

APPENDIX A
ENERGY TRADING, TRANSACTION AND RISK MANAGEMENT VENDOR LIST

Please note: This list is believed to be correct at the time of publication. For an updated list and more information at any time, subscribe to the UtiliPoint Directory of ETRM Vendors and Products, available at http://www.utilipoint.com/rci/details.asp?ProductID=1084

ABACUS SOLUTIONS, INC.
24704 Voorhees Drive
Los Altos Hills, CA 94022
650.941.1728
www.abacussolutionsinc.com

ADVANTAGE ENERGY SOLUTIONS LTD.
83 Princes Street
Edinburgh
EH2 2ER
www.aesl.co.uk

ALGORITHMICS INCORPORATED
185 Spadina Ave
Toronto, Ontario M5T 2C6
CANADA
416-217-1500
www.algorithmics.com

ALLEGRO DEVELOPMENT CORPORATION
1445 Ross Ave., Ste. 2200
Dallas, TX 75202
214-237-8000
www.allegrodevelopment.com

APX INC.
5201 Great America Pkwy
Ste. 522
Santa Clara, CA 95054
408-517-2100
www.apx.com

ASCEND ANALYTICS
Suite 100
976 Utica Circle
Boulder, CO 80304
303.415-1400
www.ascendanalytics.com

AXIOM SOFTWARE LABORATORIES INC.
67 Wall St 8
New York, NY 10005-3101
212-248-4188
www.axiomsl.com

CKLEAR
37, Coborn Street,
E3 2AB, London
U.K.
+44(0)20 89803541
www.cklear.com

C SQUARE
750 Terrado Plaza
Suite 229
Covina, CA 91723-3419
626-653-0654
www.c-square.com

CALSOFT SYSTEMS

6800 Koll Center Parkway
Suite 100
Pleasanton , CA 94566
925-249-3000
www.calsoft.co.in

CONTIGO

Blythe Valley Innovation Centre
Central Boulevard
Blythe Valley Business Park
Solihull
West Midlands
B90 8AJ
+44 (0)8458 386848
www.contigo.co.uk

DATA MANAGEMENT SOLUTIONS

707 Hunters Creek Way
Hockley, TX 77447
713-408-7835
www.dmshouston.com

DECISIONEERING, INC.

(Acquired by Hyperion 1/23/07)
1515 Arapahoe St., Ste. 1311
Denver, CO 80202
303-534-1515
www.decisioneering.com

DELTA ENERGY SOLUTION AG
Peter Merian-Strasse 90
CH - 4052 Basel
Switzerland
+41(0)61 270 84 40
www.delta-energy.com

DTN
9110 West Dodge Road, Suite 200
Omaha, NE 68114
800-485-4000
www.DTN.com

EMK3
400 Mann St.
Suite 700
Corpus Christi, TX 78401
Phone: 361-881-9326
www.emk3.com

ENCOMPASS TECHNOLOGIES
#1000 888 3rd St. S.W.,
Calgary, Alberta,
Canada T2P 5C5
(403) 237 7740
www.encompass-technologies.com

ENERGY VELOCITY
1495 Canyon Blvd Ste 100
Boulder, CO 80302
(720) 240-5500

ENERGY SOFTWORX

(Acquired by SunGard)
12100 Race Track Rd
Tampa, FL 33626-3111
(813) 814-2550
www.energysoftworx.com

ENERGY SOLUTIONS INTERNATIONAL

13831 Northwest Fwy
Houston, TX 77040
(713) 895-7722
www.energy-solutions.com

ENSYTE ENERGY SOFTWARE

770 S Post Oak Ln Ste 330
Houston, TX 77056-1974
713-622-2875
www.ensyte.com

ENWORKZ, INC.

6101 Balcones Dr Ste 300
Austin, TX 78731-4277
512-323-9118
www.enworkz.com

ENTERO

324 8th Ave. SW, Suite 1300
Calgary, AB
Canada, T2P 2Z5
403.261.1820
www.entero.com

E-SYSTEMS.NET, INC.
P.O. Box 36114,
 Birmingham, AL 35236
205-991-1518
www.e-systems.net
www.attachesystems.com

EXCELERGY
10 Maguire Rd., Ste. 111
Lexington, MA 02421
(781) 372-5000
www.excelergy.com

FINANCIAL ENGINEERING ASSOCIATES, INC.
(a wholly-owned subsidiary of Barra, Inc.)
2201 Dwight Way
Berkeley, CA 94704-2114
510-649-4640
www.fea.com

FNX LIMITED (ACQUIRED BY GLTRADE 1/16/07)
225 Washington St Ste 300
Conshohocken, PA 19428-
484-530-4400
www.fnx.com

FORTECH SOFTWARE CONSULTING, INC.,
4801 S. Lakeshore Dr. # 203
Tempe, AZ 85282
 480 237 0456
www.fortechsw.com

GLOBAL ENERGY (ACQUIRED BY VENTYX)
1470 Walnut Street, Suite 401
Boulder, CO 80302
720-221-5700
www.globalenergy.com

INNOVATIX
Crossbow House,
40 Liverpool Road,
SL1 4QZ,
UK
44 (0) 8450531694
www.innovattix.com

INTERCONTINENTALEXCHANGE, INC. (ICE)
2100 Riveredge Pkwy
Suite 500
Atlanta, GA 30328
770.857.4700
www.intcx.com

INSSINC (INVESTMENT SUPPORT SYSTEMS INC)
222 New Rd
Parsippany, NJ 07054
973-244-1661
www.inssinc.com

INTERMARK SOLUTIONS
307 East 53rd Street
6th Floor
New York, NY 10022
(212) 223 3552
www.intermarkit.com

KASE AND COMPANY, INC.
18124 Wedge Parkway
Suite 405
Reno, NV 89511
(775) 853-7037
www.kaseco.com

KIODEX
3 New York Plz FL 15
New York, NY 10004
(646) 437-3900
www.kiodex.com

LACIMA GROUP
2 Allen Center
1200 Smith Street Suite 1600
Houston, Texas 77002
(713) 353-3949
www.lacimagroup.com

LATITUDE TECHNOLOGIES
400 North Allen Drive Suite 302
Allen, TX 75013
972-747-1983
www.Latitudetech.net

LCG CONSULTING
4962 El Camino Real
#112
Los Altos, CA 94022
www.energyonline.com

LOGICAL INFORMATION MACHINES (LIM)

120 North LaSalle Street
Suite 2150
Chicago, IL 60602
(312) 456-3000
www.lim.com

LLORET DATA SYSTEMS INC

14901 Quorum Dr Ste 525
Dallas, TX 75254
(972) 238-8126
www.lloret.com

LUKENS ENERGY GROUP

2100 West Loop S Ste 1300
Houston, TX 77027
713-961-1100
www.lukensgroup.com

MINCOM

193 Turbot Street City
Brisbane Queensland
4000
Australia
61 7 3303 3333
www.mincom.com

MUREX

1270 Avenue of the Americas
Suite 1900
New York NY 10020
(212) 381 4300
www.murex.com

NEW ENERGY ASSOCIATES, LLC (ACQUIRED BY VENTYX)

400 Interstate N. Pkwy, Ste. 1400
Atlanta, GA 30339
770-779-2800
www.newenergyassoc.com

NAVITA SYSTEMS (FORMERLY KNOWN AS OM TECHNOLOGY)

199 S. Los Robles Avenue, Suite 610
Pasadena, CA 91101
www.navita.com

NEXANT

101 2nd St FL 11
San Francisco, CA 94105
(415) 369-1000
www.nexant.com

OILSPACE

PO Box 4037
Houston, TX 77210
832-263-9159
www.oilspace.com

OPEN ACCESS TECHNOLOGY INTERNATIONAL, INC. (OATI)

2300 Berkshire Ln N F
Minneapolis, MN 55441
763-553-2725
www.oatiinc.com

OPENLINK SOFTWARE, INC. (OLF)

1502 EAB Plaza
15th Floor West Tower
 Uniondale, New York. 11556
 (516) 227-6600
www.olf.com

PALMTREE BUSINESS SOLUTIONS

1430, 335 - 8 Avenue SW
Calgary, AB CANADA T2P 1C9
Phone: (403) 264-6363
www.palmtreebreeze.com

POWER COSTS, INC. (PCI)

3000 S Berry Rd Ste 100
Norman, OK 73072-7472
(405) 447-6933
www.powercosts.com

QUANTRISK CORPORATION

Miami, FL
(786) 514-6600
www.quantrisk.com

QUORUM BUSINESS SOLUTIONS (U.S.A.), INC.

2929 Briarpark Drive,
Suite 215
Houston, TX 77042
Phone: (713) 430-8600
www.qbsol.com

RAFT INTERNATIONAL

Piercy House, 7 Copthall Ave.
London
EC2R 7NJ, United Kingdom
+44-20-7847-0400
www.raftinternational.com

RCM SOLUTIONS, A DIVISION OF RISK CAPITAL MANAGEMENT PARTNERS, LLCRISK CAPITAL

1743 Wazee Street, Suite 250;
Denver, CO 80202
www.e-rcm.com

REVAL

100 Broadway, 22nd Floor
New York, NY 10005
www.reval.com

RISKADVISORY (SUBSIDIARY OF SAS)

Suite 970, 401 9 Avenue SW
Calgary, Alberta   T2P 3C5
 (403) 263-RISK (7475)
www.riskadvisory.com

ROME CORPORATION

901 S. Mopac, Suite. 110
Austin, TX 78746
(512) 347-3200
www.romecorp.com

SAKONNETT TECHNOLOGY

594 Broadway
New York, NY 10012
212 343 3170
www.sakonnettechnology.com

SAS

100 SAS Campus Drive
Cary, NC 27513-2414
(919) 677-8000
www.sas.com

SISU GROUP

2895 E 89th St
Tulsa, OK 74137-3302
(918) 495-1364
www.sisugrp.com

SOFTSMITHS

2401 Fountain View
Suite 900
Houston, TX 77057-4804
(713) 626.9184
www.softsmiths.com

SOLARC INC.

320 South Boston Avenue
Suite 600
Tulsa, Oklahoma 74103
Toll-Free: 1 (888) 594-7320
(918) 594-7320 (outside the U.S.)
www.solarc.com

SPECTRUM-PRIME SOLUTIONS L.P.

6750 West Loop South, Suite 500
Houston, TX 77401
713-662-8530
www.spectrumprime.com

SUNGARD ENERGY SOLUTIONS

1331 Lamar Street
Suite 950
Houston, Texas 77010
713.210.8000 office
713.210.8001 fax
www.sungard.com/energy

THE STRUCTURE GROUP

2000 W. Sam Houston Pkwy. South, Ste. 1600
Houston, TX 77042
Phone: 713-243-7160
www.thestructuregroup.com

TRADECAPTURE.COM

1 Landmark Square
18th Floor
Stamford, CT 06901
(203) 327-7000
www.tradecapture.com

TRIPLE POINT TECHNOLOGY

301 Riverside Ave.
Westport, CT 06880
(203) 291-7979
www.tpt.com

VISIONMONITOR SOFTWARE, LLC

11451 Katy Freeway, Suite 510,
Houston, Texas 77079
713 935 0500
www.visionmonitor.com

VIZ RISK MANAGEMENT
P.B 6216
N- 5893 Bergen
Norway
Tel: +47 55 30 28 00
www.viz.no

YELLOWJACKET SOFTWARE (ACQUIRED BY THE INTERCONTINENTAL EXCHANGE)
56 W 22nd Street, 3rd Floor
New York, NY 10010
646.202.2874
www.yellowjacketsoftware.com

ZE POWERTOOLS/ZE POWERGROUP, INC.
Unit 130
5920 No. Two Road
Richmond, BC
Canada
V7C 4R9
(604) 244-1469
www.ze.com

APPENDIX B

ENERGY TRADING, TRANSACTION AND RISK MANAGEMENT
CONSULTING COMPANIES

*Please note: This list is believed to be correct at the time of publication, however, it may
not contain all companies with an established ETRM practice.*

DELOITTE & TOUCHE LLP

1 World Financial Center
New York, NY 10281
212 436 6803
www.deloitte.com

KPMG

700 Louisiana, Ste 3200
Houston, TX 77002
713.319.2000
www.kpmg.com

MRE CONSULTING

3333 Richmond Ave., Suite 300
Houston, TX 77098
713.844.6400
www.mreconsulting.com

OPPORTUNE LLP

711 Lousiana, Suite 1770
Houston, TX 77002
713.568.4500
www.opportune.com

SAPIENT

25 First Street
Cambridge MA 02141
617.621.0200
www.sapient.com

SIRIUS SOLUTIONS
3700 Buffalo Speedway, Suite 1100
Houston, TX 77098
713.888.0488
www.siriussol.com

SUNGARD CONSULTING SERVICES
10375 Richmond Ave, Suite 700
Houston, TX 77042
713.350.1000
www.sungard.com/consultingservices/

THE STRUCTURE GROUP
2000 West Sam Houston Pkwy South, Suite 1600
Houston, TX 77042
713.243.7160
www.structuregoup.com

OTHER USEFUL RESOURCES

Other useful resources for those interested in ETRM software solutions, issues and suppliers include:

www.etrmcommunity.com – ETRM Community website provide an online community for users, buyers, developers, marketers and implementers of Energy Trading, Transaction and Risk Management (ETRM) Software facilitated by industry analysts and thought leaders – UtiliPoint International.

www.utilipoint.com – UtiliPoint International, Inc. offers the Directory of ETRM Vendors and Products from its website. The directory is updated monthly with vendor news and quarterly with other vendor and software product information. The directory is available via subscription or for one time purchase from UtiliPoint's website.

ETRM Community Blog at
http://www.etrmcommunity.com/site/modules/wordpress/ provides commentary on salient industry issues.

UtiliPoint's European Blog at
http://www.utilipointeuropeblog.com provides commentary on salient industry issues affecting the European energy markets

Additionally, UtiliPoint publishes a variety of free white papers and research for purchase at its website.

SPONSOR INFORMATION

ABOUT DELOITTE & TOUCHE LLP

DELOITTE & TOUCHE'S ENERGY & RESOURCES PRACTICE

The energy industry specialists in Deloitte & Touche LLP's Regulatory & Capital Markets Consulting practice offer a comprehensive range of services to help clients assess, design, and implement energy transacting and risk management solutions in the wholesale and retail sectors. Our team of approximately 200 experienced professionals has a proven track record in helping some of the world's largest integrated oil companies, major utilities, and leading financial firms to seize new opportunities while managing volatility and risk. Leveraging the deep industry experience and strong business and technical skills of our staff, we provide an integrated suite of services that spans risk strategy, technology and business process, regulatory compliance, cι᷈ advisory, accounting, and quantitative analytics.

Contact Information

For more information about Deloitte & Touche's contribution to this text (Chapter 12) or to access Deloitte & Touche's additional tools and methodology for testing or ETRM implementation, please contact:

Roger Schaffland
Energy & Resources
Director
Deloitte & Touche LLP
1 World Financial Center
New York, NY 10281
Office: +1 212 436 6803
Email: rschaffland@deloitte.com

ABOUT SAPIENT

SAPIENT'S TRADING AND RISK MANAGEMENT PRACTICE

Sapient, a business innovator, helps clients achieve extraordinary results from their customer relationships, business operations, and technology. Leveraging Wall Street-caliber talent distributed across a global workforce, an innovative approach, and disciplined execution, Sapient's Trading and Risk Management practice has helped clients support business growth, optimize margins, and increase operational flexibility.

For more information, please contact:

Sapient
25 First Street
Cambridge, MA 02141
www.sapient.com
+1 617 761 1676
info@sapient.com

ABOUT THE STRUCTURE GROUP

STRUCTURE'S PREMIER ETRM PRACTICE

With deep ETRM expertise across a wide variety of energy clients, Structure is the premier solutions company offering consulting services to participants in the global energy markets. Our consulting service lines address a broad range of business needs across the front, mid and back office. Structure has the experience to implement a holistic front-to-back vision across your trading and risk management systems, processes and organization.

For additional information on Structure's ETRM services in North America, email: Angela Ryan, Consulting Practice Director at angela.ryan@thestructuregroup.com or Baris Ertan, Consulting Practice Senior Manager at baris.ertan@thestructuregroup.com.

For additional information on Structure's ETRM services in Europe, email: Mohamed Mansour, European Wholesale Trading Practice Director at mohamed.mansour@thestructuregroup.co.uk

Made in the USA